The Star of Bethle
John

The Star of Bethlehem: The New Evidence
John C. Iannone

THE STAR OF BETHLEHEM:

THE NEW EVIDENCE

John C. Iannone

Psalm 19: 1-3

"The heavens declare the glory of God;

the skies proclaim the work of his hands.

Day after day they pour forth speech;

night after night they reveal knowledge.

They have no speech, they use no words;

no sound is heard from them."

DEDICATION

This book is dedicated to my wife Kim; my son John
Paul and his new bride Kelly; my daughter
Samantha and her husband Camden

and

The four most beautiful grandchildren ever:

Landen (7); Ava (6) and Gianna Marie (Gigi) (5)

and one on the way!

Note: The Biblical quotes used in this book are taken
from

THE NEW ILLUSTRATED VERSION (NIV) OF

THE OLD and NEW TESTAMENT

Revision 1: Dec. 31, 2013

CREDITS

A special thanks goes to **Rick Larson** for his inspiring DVD: *The Star of Bethlehem* produced by Stephen McEveety (The Passion of the Christ) (www.bethlehemstar.net) and to:

Barry Setterfield for his inspiring DVD: *The Christmas Star: Do Astronomy and History Support the Bible?* (produced by Freedom Films and Video) and to all the writers who have inspired me to pursue the truth.

The Star of Bethlehem: The New Evidence
John C. Iannone

TABLE OF CONTENTS

The Star of Bethlehem: The New Evidence
John C. Iannone

The Star of Bethlehem: The New Evidence
John C. Iannone

INTRODUCTION

As a young boy raised in an Italian neighborhood in New York, my family and I attended the beautiful Church of St. Barbara. The parish always had a grand display at Christmas featuring the manger with animals, shepherds, Magi and most importantly Mary and Joseph with the infant Jesus. Above them was the Star of Bethlehem.

For me, it was a matter of simple faith that the Star of Bethlehem, which we sometimes called "The Christmas Star," was a real heavenly phenomenon that actually guided the Magi to Bethlehem. I didn't understand it but I was always inspired by it and never questioned it.

In my college years at the Catholic University in Washington, I worked on my Masters in Religious Studies and then went to Fordham University and Union Theological Seminary where the knowledge of my faith increased but where I also had to study those that thought differently about Christian mysteries. Things were not as simple as they were as a child and I entered the world of controversy and felt a need to understand my faith in order to defend it.

There were those who completely denied Christianity. Of more surprise to me, though, were those Christians who accepted the Christian faith but said that the Star of Bethlehem was a myth, a fanciful story with no basis in fact. To them, it was just a nice Christmas tradition with no basis in science and history.

Naturally, I found their position disappointing, but it persuaded me to delve into this fascinating mystery of my faith. I studied others who studied the Star and paid particular attention to the historians and astronomers who not only believed in the reality of the Star but presented fascinating new and old evidence for the true existence of the event.

It is the objective of this book to carefully build on the compelling historical and scientific work of modern astronomy that, standing on the shoulders of giants like Copernicus, Johannes Kepler, Galileo and Sir Isaac Newton, allowed modern computer experts to use what they learned to re-create the skies around the time we believe Jesus was born. It is often said that a picture is worth a thousand words and you will view the evidence in this book both in writing and visually. I hope you will find the evidence as compelling as I did in building the case for not only when Jesus was born, but in affirming the reality of the event we call the Star of Bethlehem that accompanied His conception and birth.

Most important, I hope to leave the reader with the incredible sense of awe when one begins to understand how God viewed the stars of the universe He created. He ordered the movement of the stars to come together in conjunction with the planets to mark a pivotal, unfathomable, event in our history – the birth of His Son Jesus.

Thank you

John C. Iannone

December 2013

The Star of Bethlehem: The New Evidence
John C. Iannone

CHAPTER ONE

GOD'S MAJESTY – CREATING & ORDERING THE STARS

"Joy to the World , the Lord is come!

Let earth receive her King;

Let every heart prepare Him room,

And Heaven and nature sing,

And Heaven and nature sing,

And Heaven, and Heaven, and nature sing.

Joy to the World, the Savior reigns!

Let men their songs employ;

While fields and floods, rocks, hills and plains

Repeat the sounding joy,

Repeat the sounding joy,

Repeat, repeat, the sounding joy."

(The words are by English hymn writer Isaac Watts, based on Psalm 98 in the Bible and was first published in 1719. Isaac Watts was an English hymn writer, theologian and logician.

The Book of Job:

Many scholars agree that *The Book Job* is the oldest book in the Bible, written by an Israelite about 1500 B.C. *The Book of Job* might be, arguably, one of the oldest books in the world. It is older than Genesis, though Genesis covers older material. Written before the time of Abraham, Isaac and Jacob, the Book of Job boldly announces that God is the creator of the heavens and claims dominion over the stars. He has set in motion the "laws of the heavens" and takes pride in His creation.

So, the sacred Scriptures begin with an affirmation of God's power over the creation and ordering of the stars.

JOB 9:*9*

"He is the Maker of the Bear and Orion,

The Pleiades and the constellations of the south."

JOB 38: 31-32:

> *"Can you bind the chains of the Pleiades?*
>
> *Can you loosen Orion's belt?*
>
> *Can you bring forth the constellations in their seasons?*
>
> *Or lead out the Bear with its cubs?*
>
> *Do you know the laws of the heavens?*
>
> *Can you set up God's dominion over the earth?"*

It is most interesting, even prophetic, that written some 3,500 years ago, Job is talking about the "laws of the heavens" and foreshadowing the discovery of the incredible mathematics and laws of physics and astronomy that govern the motions of the planets and stars. Some 3,000 years later, scholars such as Copernicus, Johannes Kepler, Galileo and Sir Isaac Newton would come to understand that, contrary to the teachings of the Greek philosopher Aristotle and the Roman astronomer Ptolemy, the Sun is the center of our solar system. They would define the "laws of planetary motion" and the "general laws of motion" which would open up the exciting modern "space age" and our ability to go to the Moon, send Space Shuttles into orbit and thrust probes to other planets with incredible accuracy. Further, these discoveries would enable us to revisit the movement of planets in the past.

Reversing Time:

The advances in computer science that crunch millions of pieces of data have allowed Astronomers to actually use computers to re-create the position of the stars at the time of Jesus' birth and open new vistas in our understanding of the words of the Gospels of Matthew and Luke regarding the conception, birth and earliest life of Jesus.

In the Book of **Isaiah 40:26 we read:**

"Lift up your eyes and look to the heavens:

Who created all these?

He who brings out the starry host one by one

And calls forth each of them by name.

Because of His great power and mighty strength,

Not one of them is missing."

The Star of Bethlehem: The New Evidence
John C. Iannone

In the Psalms, we find the beautiful prayer of David, the first King of Israel around 1000 B.C.

Psalms 19: 1-4,

> *"The heavens declare the glory of God;*
>
> *The skies proclaim the work of his hands.*
>
> *Day after day they pour forth speech;*
>
> *Night after night they reveal knowledge.*
>
> *They have no speech, they use no words;*
>
> *No sound is heard from them.*
>
> *Yet their voice goes out into all the earth,*
>
> *Their words to the ends of the world.*
>
> *In the heavens God has pitched a tent for the sun."*

Even more compelling, we see that the ordering of the planets and Star at the time of Jesus' birth (which we have come to know as the Star of Bethlehem) was the unfathomable work of the hand of God.

The Hubble Telescope:

Modern research in astronomy, with the aid of high-tech instruments such as the Hubble Space Telescope

The Star of Bethlehem: The New Evidence
John C. Iannone

(HST), has opened new worlds in our understanding of the universe. The Hubble Space Telescope was carried into orbit by the Space Shuttle Discovery in 1990. In low Earth orbit, Hubble's four main instruments observe in the near ultraviolet, visible, and near infrared.

Unimpeded by the pollution, light, moisture and clouds of Earth's atmosphere, Hubble allows a deep view into space. Many Hubble observations and other telescopic examinations from mountaintop Observatories around the world have led to breakthroughs in astrophysics, such as accurately determining the rate of expansion of the universe and the utter depth of the heavens which continue to reveal new secrets.

The Star of Bethlehem: The New Evidence
John C. Iannone

(The Hubble Space Telescope. "Edwin Hubble, by his inspired use of the largest telescope of his time, the 100 inch reflector on the Mount Wilson Observatory, revolutionized our knowledge of the size, structure, and properties of the universe. Hubble's observations proved that galaxies are 'island universes"). (www.nasa.gov)

The Vastness of the Universe: God's Hand

Ethan Siegel, a theoretical astrophysicist living in Portland, Oregon, has estimated that there are over 176 billion galaxies and likely many more yet to be discovered. Multiply that by the number of stars and planets in each of the galaxies and the number is staggering and unimaginable.

And yet God claims dominion over them. He creates them, names them and orders their movement.

It is mind boggling and beyond human conception that He has created and set the stars and planets into motion in a precise clockwork-like movement that would culminate in the alignment of the King Star (Regulus) in the Constellation of Leo the Lion (the symbol of the tribe of Judah from which the Messiah would come) and the King Planet (Jupiter) in such a way as to form the phenomenon of the Star of Bethlehem at the conception (Incarnation) of Jesus and continue the phenomenon with the alignment of Jupiter and Venus near Regulus at His birth (Nativity). Venus, the brightest planet in our solar system, is the goddess of love and the Mother Star symbolic of Mary, the Mother of Jesus which came into a startling conjunction with the King Planet Jupiter in June, 2 B.C.

It is the objective of our study in this book to demonstrate that this is precisely what happened after looking closely at history, science, astronomy and biblical research.

CHAPTER TWO

BEGINNINGS: THE TRIBE OF JUDAH & THE CONSTELLATION OF LEO THE LION

"It came upon the midnight clear,

That glorious song of old,

From angels bending near the earth,

To touch their harps of gold:

Peace on the earth, goodwill to men

From heavens all gracious King!

The world in solemn stillness lay

To hear the angels sing.

Still through the cloven skies they come,

With peaceful wings unfurled;

And still their heavenly music floats

O'er all the weary world:

Above its sad and lowly plains

They bend on hovering wing,

And ever o'er its Babel sounds

The blessed angels sing."

("It Came Upon the Midnight Clear" is a poem and Christmas carol written by Edmund Sears, pastor of the Unitarian Church in Wayland, Massachusetts in 1849).

Beginnings: The Tribe of Judah:

To properly lay the foundation for understanding the significance of The Nativity Star, we will begin with the importance of the Tribe of Judah in the history of Israel and the Tribe's symbol, the Constellation of Leo the Lion.

In the ***Book of*** *Genesis 48: 9-10* we are told that the Messiah will come from the Tribe of Judah:

"You are a lion's cub, Judah;

You return from the prey, my son.

Like a lion he crouches and lies down,

Like a lioness—who dares to rouse him?

The scepter will not depart from Judah,

Nor the ruler's staff from between his feet,

Until he to whom it belongs shall come

And the obedience of the nations shall be his."

Judah is compared to a lion and is the Tribe from which the Messiah will come.

The Twelve Tribes of Israel:

We will first give a brief synopsis of the Twelve Tribes of Israel and the significance of the symbol of the tribe of Judah: the **Constellation of Leo the Lion** and its principal and largest Star, the King Star **Regulus.**

The twelve tribes are descended from the sons and grandsons of the Jewish forefather Jacob and are called "Israel" from Jacob's name given to him by God. The twelve tribes are as follows: **Reuben, Simeon, Judah, Issachar, Zebulon, Benjamin, Dan, Naphtali, Gad, Asher, Ephraim and Manasseh.**

Jacob and his family went down to Egypt and the people grew and multiplied and became the Israelite People. One of Jacob's sons, **Joseph**, became a viceroy of the Pharaoh, who then began to oppress the Israelites.

Moses was then chosen by God to rescue the Israelites from Egypt. The nation numbered "600,000 men on foot" which is usually understood to be military-aged men excluding women and children.

An article in *Encyclopaedia Judaica* states that:

> "At Mount Sinai, the Israelite nation is given its laws and regulations - the **Torah** - and affirms their covenant with God. After wandering for 40 years in the desert under the leadership of Moses, the twelve tribes enter the land of Canaan with **Joshua** in command."

> "After conquering the land, each tribe was allotted an individual territory to settle. During this period of settlement, and the subsequent period of the Judges, there was no predetermined pattern of leadership among the tribes though various crises forced the tribes into cooperative action against common enemies."

Eventually, the tribe sought to establish a monarch and **David** became the first King. Of significance is the fact that he was of the Tribe of Judah.

The alliance of the twelve tribes is believed to have grown from the organization of independent tribes, or groups of tribes, forced together for historical, often military, reasons. The confederation of the twelve tribes was primarily religious, based upon belief in the one "God of Israel" with whom the tribes had made a covenant and whom they worshiped at a common sacral center as the "people of the Lord."

The Lion of Judah:

The Lion of Judah is an ancient symbol. The sign represents the Israelite tribe of Judah throughout the Old Testament. The symbol of the Lion dates back to the tribe's patriarch **Jacob**, who referred to his son **Judah** as 'Gur Aryeh' or 'the young lion' (Genesis 49:9).

In Christianity, the Lion of Judah epithet is used to refer to Jesus Christ. Revelations 5:5 in the New Testament states:

> *"Then one of the elders said to me, 'Do not weep! See, the Lion of the tribe of Judah, the Root of David, has triumphed. He is able to open the scroll and its seven seals.' "*

The symbol is read and understood as a direct reference to Jesus, where he is regarded as the 'Lion of the Tribe' and 'Root of David'.

The Bible reveals the following instances when Jesus was referred to as the Lion of Judah:

Gen 49:8-9: The Lion of Judah, a strong fighter against the enemy.

Hebrews 7: 14 St. Paul states: *"'For it is clear that our Lord descended from Judah, and in regard to that tribe Moses said nothing about priests."*

Note: The ancient tribe of Levi prepared priests. Judah, however, was the tribe of the Kings. Jesus is a descendant of the Tribe of Judah. King David, an ancestor of Jesus, was also from Judah's lineage and hence, Jesus is referred to as the 'Root of David' (1 Kings 2:45).

Samuel tells David:

"Your throne shall be established forever." (2 Sam. 7:16)

The Tribe of Judah and the Constellation of the Lion:

The tribe of Judah was assigned to the Zodiac house of Leo the Lion. Judah carried the symbol of the lion, reflecting on Earth what the Zodiac sign of Leo the Lion declared in the heavens.

Constellations and the Zodiac:

What is the Zodiac? The Zodiac is closely tied to how the Earth moves through the heavens. The signs are derived from 12 constellations that mark out the path on which the sun appears to travel over the course of a year.

As the Earth orbits the sun, the sun appears to pass in front of different constellations. Much like the moon appears in a slightly different place in the sky each night, the location of the sun relative to distant background stars drifts in an easterly direction from day to day. It's not that the sun is actually moving. The motion is entirely an illusion caused by the Earth's own motion around our sun.

The Twelve Constellations constituting the Zodiac were defined by the Roman astronomer **Ptolemy** in his *Almagest,* an astronomical manual written about 150 A.D. by Ptolemy (Claudius Ptolemaeus of Alexandria). It served as the basic guide for Islamic and European astronomers until about the beginning of the 17th century.

THE 12 TRIBES OF ISRAEL

http://www.jewishvirtuallibrary.org -
jsource/Judaism/tribemap.htm

THE CONSTELLATIONS OF THE ZODIAC

Aries: The Ram

Taurus: The Bull

Gemini: The Twins

Cancer: The Crab

Leo: The Lion

Virgo: The Virgin/Maiden

Libra: The Scales

Scorpio: The Scorpion

Sagittarius: The (Centaur) Archer

Capricorn: "Goat-horned" (The Sea-Goat)

Aquarius: The Water-Bearer

Pisces: The Fish

http://www.jewishvirtuallibrary.org

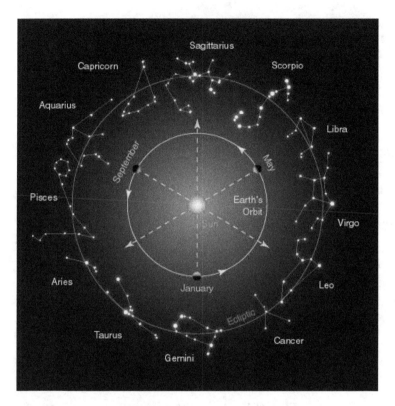

Zoroastrian (Persian) - Astrology & Cosmology: http://zoroastrianastrology.blogspot.com - **p/houses-of-zodiac.html.**

The Constellation of Leo the Lion and the King Star Regulus:

What are constellations? A simple definition is that a Constellation is a group of stars that, when seen from Earth, form a pattern to the human eye. There are 88 constellations.

Another definition is that a Constellation "in astronomy is any of certain groupings of stars that were imagined—at least by those who named them—to form conspicuous configurations of objects or creatures in the sky." One of these is the Constellation of Leo the Lion.

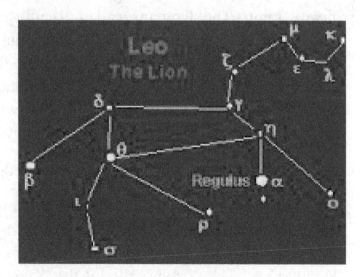

(The Constellation of Leo, the Lion). Note Regulus, the brightest star in the Constellation).

The Star of Bethlehem: The New Evidence
John C. Iannone

When ancient astronomers looked to the heavens, the pattern of stars seen in the above chart resembled a Lion. The brightest of these stars is **Regulus, or The King Star.** Regulus becomes most important in our story as the King Star of the Constellation of Leo the Lion. The Constellation of Leo was chosen in ancient Israel to be the constellation representing the Tribe of Judah.

Rick Larson, writer of *"The Starry Dance"* notes that Regulus takes its name from the word root which yields our word "regal."

> "The Babylonians called Regulus *Sharu*, which means 'king.' The Romans called Regulus *Rex* which means 'king' in Latin. So, to start things, at the beginning of the new Jewish year, the Planet of Kings met the Star of Kings. This conjunction may have indicated kingship in a forceful way to a Babylonian magus." (www.behlehemstar.net)

According to the Associates for Scriptural Knowledge:

> "Regulus was known as 'the King.' The Romans referred to it as "Rex," which means "King" in Latin. In Arabia the star was known as the "Kingly One." The Greeks called it the "King Star." Of all the stars in the heavens, Regulus was universally associated by the ancient astrologers with the attributes of greatness and power. It is

located practically on the ecliptic (the path which the Sun takes in traversing the heavens). It was thought that this position made it of special importance to the Sun. According to astrologers the Sun ruled the heavens. Thus, the major star closest to the ecliptic of the "ruling" Sun was Regulus. This close relationship to the Sun made Regulus a "royal star," the one most associated with the conception or birth of kings. It was the star denoting rulership."

The King Star Regulus in the Constellation of Leo the Lion (the symbol of Judah) was to play a vital role in understanding the celestial events which we call The Star of Bethlehem. Regulus is the brightest star in the constellation Leo and one of the brightest stars in the nighttime sky.

Regulus is approximately 77.5 light years from Earth. This is a mind-boggling distance as light travels at 186,000 miles per second!

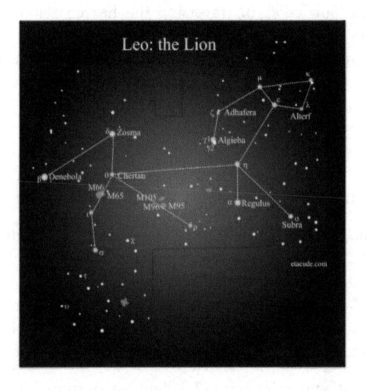

Leo: the Lion

(http://rlv.zcache.com - **Leo_the_Lion_constellation**)

The Associates for Scriptural Knowledge make another important statement:

> "With this in mind, we should recall the Prophecy of Balaam recorded by Moses. He spoke about a 'star' to rise in Israel that would be connected with rulership or dominion."

The Star of Bethlehem: The New Evidence
John C. Iannone

> 'A star shall come out of Jacob and a scepter [ruling rod] shall rise out of Israel.' " Book of Numbers 22-23.

Further:

> "The arrangement of the verses in the prophecy shows that the 'star' is connected with a 'scepter.' This suggests that the star would symbolically represent 'dominion.' This is made clear in the following verse of the prophecy:

> *"Out of Jacob shall come he that shall have dominion."*

> This is why the scepter is associated with the star. It was the tribe of Judah (Leo, the Lion) that was prophesied to possess this scepter in Israel. *'Judah is a lion's whelp ... he crouched as a lion ... the scepter shall not depart from Judah until Shiloh come.'* Since the Bible talks of the star, a scepter, and Judah (the Lion, Leo), the only star in the heavens that fits this combination of factors mentioned by Balaam is the star Regulus (the King star)."

Roman Speculation:

It is interesting that both **Tacitus** and **Suetonius** (Roman historians) noted that:

"Speculation was rife at the time that the ruler of the world would emerge from Judah – an expectation that Flavius Josephus applied to (the Emperor) Vespasian, consequently finding his way into the latter's favor." (Josephus: *The Jewish Wars*, iii, 399-408).

Would the Conjunction of Jupiter and Regulus alone trigger the Magi to start on their Journey?

Rick Larson notes that this is not likely. It was the later Conjunction of Jupiter and Venus (the King and His Virgin Mother) near Regulus nine months later at the birth of Jesus that acted as the "trigger" which told them that a King was born. The earlier conjunction of Jupiter and Regulus at the conception of Jesus was the conjunction that alerted them to watch the skies.

Larson notes:

"Jupiter glides slowly past Regulus about every 12 years. Let's assume our magus enjoyed a 50 year career, say from age 20 to 70. We don't know how old the Magi were, but if our man was in the second half of his career, he might have seen such a pass two or three times before. Jupiter's orbit wobbles relative to Regulus, so not every conjunction is as close as the one he saw in 3 B.C. Perhaps our magus recorded this event with some interest, but it is hard to imagine great excitement. Not from this alone."

(Rick   Larson   "The   Starry   Dance."
www.behlehemstar.net)

Larson believes that the later conjunction of the Planet Venus (representing Mary – the Mother of Jesus) and the Planet Jupiter (the King Planet) under the canopy of Regulus (the King Star) occurred at the birth, the Nativity, and set the Magi in motion to follow the Star. We accept this premise and will demonstrate it in this book.

(In center of screen: The conjunction of the King Planet Jupiter just below the King Star Regulus in the Constellation of Leo the Lion on September 17, 3 B.C. at 6:30 A.M. symbolizing the conception of the Messiah. www.CyberSky.com)

The Star of Bethlehem: The New Evidence
John C. Iannone

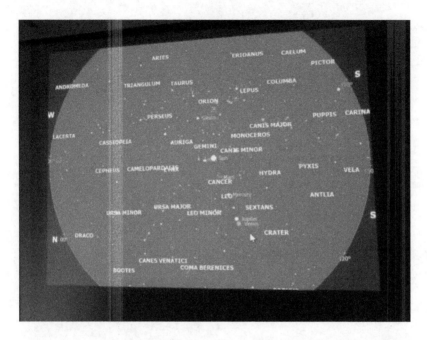

(The conjunction of the King Planet Jupiter with Venus – a symbol of Mary – adjacent to the King Star Regulus in the Constellation of Leo the Lion in June 17, 2 B.C. at the birth of Jesus. Photo from Astronomy program www.CyberSky.com).

The Star of Bethlehem: The New Evidence
John C. Iannone

CHAPTER THREE

JUPITER AND VENUS – THE PLANETS IN CONJUNCTION

(The Planet Jupiter by www.NASA.gov. This photo of Jupiter was taken on Sept. 20, 2010 when Jupiter made its closest approach to Earth since 1963).

The Star of Bethlehem: The New Evidence
John C. Iannone

"The first Noel the angel did say

Was to certain poor shepherds in fields as they lay:

In fields where they lay keeping their sheep

On a cold winter's night that was so deep.

Noel Noel Noel Noel

Born is the King of Israel.

They looked up and saw a star

Shining in the east beyond them far:

And to the earth it gave great light

And so it continued both day and night.

Noel Noel Noel Noel

Born is the King of Israel.

And by the light of that same star

Three wise men came from the country far;

To seek for a King was their intent,

And to follow the star wherever it went.

Noel, Noel, Noel, Noel,

Born is the King of Israel."

The Star of Bethlehem: The New Evidence
John C. Iannone

(*The First Noel* is a traditional classical English carol, most likely from the 18th century. The word *Noel* comes from the French word *Noël* meaning Christmas which in turn comes from the Latin word *natalis* which translates as birthday").

Jupiter – The King Planet:

To understand the phenomenon of the Star of Bethlehem, we start by focusing on the planet Jupiter, the largest of the planets in our Solar System.

The ancient Greeks named the planet after Zeus, the king of the Greek Pantheon.

The Romans named the planet after Jupiter, the supreme god of the Roman Pantheon.

> "Jupiter is the supreme god of the Roman pantheon, called *dies pater*, 'shining father.' He is a god of light and sky, and protector of the state and its laws. He is a son of Saturn and brother of Neptune and Juno.... The Romans worshipped him especially as Jupiter Optimus Maximus (all-good, all-powerful). This name refers not only to his rulership over the universe, but also to his function as the god of the state who distributes laws, controls the realm and makes his will

known through oracles. His English name is Jove."
(www.pantheon.org)

Jupiter is the most massive planet in our solar system, more than twice as massive as all the other planets combined. Had it been about 80 times more massive, it would have actually become a star instead of a planet. Its atmosphere resembles that of the sun, made up mostly of hydrogen and helium. With four large moons and many smaller moons in orbit around it, Jupiter by itself forms a kind of miniature solar system. All told, the immense volume of Jupiter could hold more than 1,300 Earths.

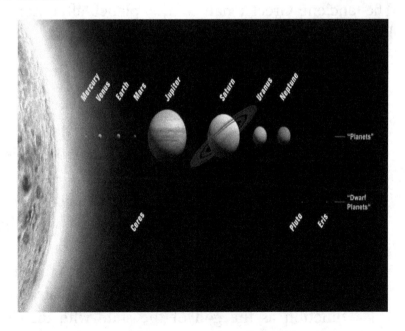

(Jupiter is 483 million miles from the Sun and 370 million miles from Earth. It takes 12 Earth years for Jupiter to orbit the Sun).

How is Jupiter Related to our Story?

Events in the ancient skies from approximately September 3 B.C. to June of 2 B.C., as recreated by astronomers, show that there was an alignment in the sky of Regulus and Jupiter at the conception of Jesus which created a breath-taking appearance of a large star – one which would catch the watchful eyes of the Magi. They would follow the star (or conjunction of planet and the star) after His birth nine months later in June 2 B.C. when Jupiter and Venus, the brightest planet, came in conjunction under the canopy of Leo the Lion.

(This image gives perspective on the size of Earth as compared to Jupiter. Jupiter's massive size inspired the Roman's to call it The King Planet). www.amazon.com

The Planet Venus–The Brightest Planet in the Solar System:

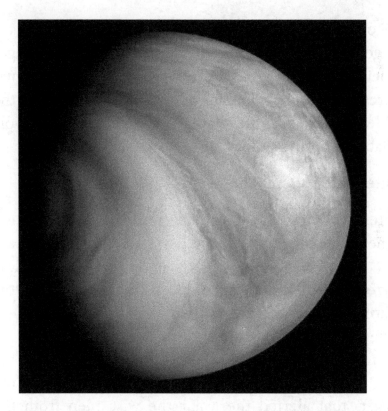

www.space.com/44-venus-second-planet-from-the-sun-brightest- planet-in-solar-system.html

The planet Venus is the second planet from the Sun and is the brightest planet in the Solar System as its clouds reflect the Sun's light. It is 68 million miles from the Sun and 24 million miles from its neighbor – Earth. It takes .62 years to circle the Sun.

The Significance of Venus:

In Roman mythology the planet was called **Venus** – the goddess of beauty. In Greek mythology, this bright planet was called **Aphrodite** – the goddess of love. Interesting, the Babylonians identified Venus with the goddess **Ishtar** and the planet played a significant role in Babylonian cosmology.

Jupiter, Venus and The Magi:

Jupiter, the King Planet, was the most important planet to the Babylonians which was associated with Marduk – the god of Babylon. (burro.cwre.edu/stu/advanced/pre20th/ancients_babylon on.html). It would seem then that a conjunction of Jupiter and Venus would catch the eyes of Babylonian astronomers/astrologers, especially in proximity to the King Star Regulus. This conjunction was likely the "trigger" that alerted the Magi, the wise men from the east, to seek the birthplace of a new King. They learned about the prophesies of the Messiah from the Prophet Daniel, the Jewish prophet taken into captivity by the Babylonians in the 6th century B.C.

The Star of Bethlehem: The New Evidence
John C. Iannone

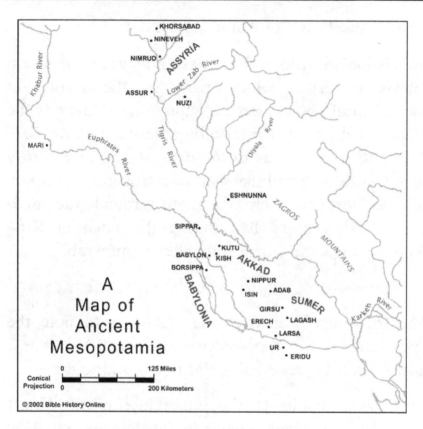

(Babylon, between the Tigris and Euphrates Rivers, was the home of the ancient Sumerians and then the Babylonians. It is to the east of Israel. It is likely the place from which the Magi departed. To the east of Babylon are the Zagros Mountains which separate the ancient Persians/Parthians from the Babylonians).

http://www.bible-history.com/maps/maps/map_ancient_mesopotamia.html

The Venus Tablet of Ammisaduqa:

In Babylonian history, there were numerous cuneiform tablets preserved which refer to the record of astronomical observation of Venus. One of these is the **Venus Tablet of Ammisaduqa** *(Enuma Anu Enlil* Tablet 63 translated as *In the days of Anu and Enlil,* a long text dealing with Babylonian astrology). The origin of this text is likely dated to around the mid-seventeenth century B.C. during the reign of **King Ammisaduqa**, the fourth ruler after Hammurabi.

(www.en.wikipedia.org/wiki/Venus_tablet_of_Ammisaduqa)

The main significance of this Tablet is to note the appearance and disappearance of the planet Venus as it goes from being an evening star to a morning star.

This Tablet points to the importance of the Planet Venus and the Planet Jupiter in Babylonian mythology and astronomy. The Magi, likely from Babylon, found great significance in this conjunction of Venus and Jupiter in June 2 B.C. even though they did not know about Mary, the Mother of Jesus (later signified by Venus) and Jesus (later signified by Jupiter). They knew of prophesies of a Messiah from the Jewish Prophet Daniel and believed a King was born. They followed the star which was a conjunction of the very bright planet (Venus) and the largest planet Jupiter – appearing as one in the heavens.

The Star of Bethlehem: The New Evidence
John C. Iannone

(The Venus Tablet of King Ammisáduqa - cuneiform tablet 63)

****

The Star of Bethlehem: The New Evidence
John C. Iannone

CHAPTER FOUR

THE NATIVITY AND THE GOSPEL OF LUKE

"Angels we have heard on high

Sweetly singing o'er the plains,

And the mountains in reply

Echoing their joyous strains.

Gloria, in excelsis Deo! Gloria, in excelsis Deo!

Shepherds, why this jubilee?

Why your joyous strains prolong?

What the gladsome tidings be

Which inspire your heavenly song?

Come to Bethlehem and see

Christ whose birth the angels sing;

Come, adore on bended knee,

53

Christ the Lord, the newborn King."

(A traditional French carol known as Les Anges dans nos Campagnes - literally, "Angels in our countryside"- composed by an unknown author in Languedoc, France).

The Traditional Nativity Scene – Correcting a Misconception:

It is interesting that many, if not most, Christians think of the Nativity scene as including the Shepherds and Angels at the Manger accompanied by the three Kings, the Magi, from the East bearing gifts.

In attempting to determine the exact time of the birth of Jesus and correlating His birth with celestial events, we need to correct a misconception. The two Gospels that discuss Jesus' birth and infancy are **The Gospels of Matthew and Luke**. Each gives a different perspective.

Luke, for example, speaks of the Shepherds and Angels at the Manger but does not mention the Wise Men from the East (The Magi) or the Star. Matthew, on the other hand, speaks more of Jesus as a child, a toddler, and the <u>visit of the Magi to Jesus' home (not manger) at a later time</u>. He does not mention Shepherds and Angels. Matthew also talks about the Star and Luke does not mention this. The presence of Magi at the Manger grew in tradition, but it does not appear from Matthew that the Magi were at the Manger with the Shepherds.

By examining the two Gospels, we get a better view of the timing of events that can help establish a correlation with events in the heavens leading us to the Star. Let us begin with the Gospel of Luke regarding the birth of Jesus in a Manger involving Angels and Shepherds.

THE GOSPEL OF LUKE 2: 1-21

1 "In those days Caesar Augustus issued a decree that a census should be taken of the entire Roman world.

2 (This was the first census that took place while Quirinius was governor of Syria).

3 and everyone went to their own town to register.

4 So Joseph also went up from the town of Nazareth in Galilee to Judea, to Bethlehem the town of David, because he belonged to the house and line of David.

5 He went there to register with Mary, who was pledged to be married to him and was expecting a child.

6 While they were there, the time came for the baby to be born,

7 and she gave birth to her firstborn, a son. She wrapped him in clothes and placed him in a manger, because there was no guest room available for them.

8 And there were shepherds living out in the fields nearby, keeping watch over their flocks at night.

9 An angel of the Lord appeared to them, and the glory of the Lord shone around them, and they were terrified.

10 But the angel said to them, "Do not be afraid. I bring you good news that will cause great joy for all the people.

11 Today in the town of David a Savior has been born to you; he is the Messiah, the Lord.

12 This will be a sign to you: You will find a baby wrapped in clothes and lying in a manger."

13 Suddenly a great company of the heavenly host appeared with the angel, praising God and saying,

14 Glory to God in the highest heaven, and on earth peace to those on whom his favor rests.

(www.rentonchristian.org)

15 When the angels had left them and gone into heaven, the shepherds said to one another, "Let's go to Bethlehem and see this thing that has happened, which the Lord has told us about."

16 So they hurried off and found Mary and Joseph, and the baby, who was lying in the manger.

17 When they had seen him, they spread the word concerning what had been told them about this child,

18 and all who heard it were amazed at what the shepherds said to them.

19 But Mary treasured up all these things and pondered them in her heart.

20 The shepherds returned, glorifying and praising God for all the things they had heard and seen which were just as they had been told.

21 On the eighth day, when it was time to circumcise the child, he was named Jesus, the name the angel had given him before he was conceived."

The Star of Bethlehem: The New Evidence
John C. Iannone

We note some important items in Luke's account:

Verse 1: Caesar Augustus was Emperor of Rome.

Caesar Augustus (Octavian) was the nephew of Julius Caesar. Born in 63 BC., he was the founder of the Roman Empire and its first Emperor, ruling from 27 BC until his death in 14 AD. Caesar Augustus brought organization, order, and stability to the Roman world – the Pax Romana. His establishment of a professional army ensured that insurrections were put down quickly. He changed the way governors were appointed in the provinces, which reduced greed and extortion. Ironically, the peace and order established by Augustus and maintained by his successors helped in the spread of Christianity. The extensive network of Roman roads made travel easier and a standard currency enabled trade and commerce. www.christianity.about.com.

The Pax Romana:

Pax Romana is Latin for "Roman Peace." The Pax Romana lasted from about 27 B.C. (with Augustus) until A.D. 180. The name Augustus meant "one worthy of admiration."

The Star of Bethlehem: The New Evidence
John C. Iannone

As Joseph Ratzinger (Pope Emeritus Benedict XVI) noted:

> "In the inscription at Priene, he (Augustus) is called Saviour, Redeemer (soter). This title, which literature ascribed to Zeus . . . is reserved in the Greek translation of the Old Testament to God alone. For Augustus too, there was a divine ring to it: the Emperor ushered in a changed world, a new era." *The Infancy Narratives - Jesus of Nazareth, p .60.*

For the first time, there was a government and an empire that spanned the known world. It was a period when there was a common law, a universal language, peace on the high seas, Roman roads which allowed travel, currency, construction of aqueducts and bridges and a security that united the Empire. The Pax Romana was in effect at the time of the birth of Jesus and helped in the expansion of Christianity.

Pax Romana was the long period of relative peace and minimal expansion by military force experienced by the Roman Empire in the 1st and 2nd centuries AD. Since it was established by Caesar Augustus it is sometimes called Pax Augusta.

The Star of Bethlehem: The New Evidence
John C. Iannone

The Roman Empire during the Pax Romana
http://www.usu.edu.com

(Mary and Joseph register for the census before Governor Quirinius. From a Byzantine mosaic c. 1315).

Verse 2: Caesar Augustus orders a census to be taken of the entire Roman world while Quirinius was governor (Legate) of Syria.

Some authors maintain that the Census of Quirinius refers to the enrollment of the Roman provinces of Syria and Judaea for tax purposes taken in the year 6/7 B.C. The Census was taken during the reign of Augustus (27 B.C. - 14 A.D when Publius Sulpicius Quirinius was appointed governor of Syria.

The Star of Bethlehem: The New Evidence
John C. Iannone

Correcting a Misconception:

"The Jewish historian Josephus recorded that in the year 6-7, after the exile of Herod Archelaus (one of the sons and successors of Herod the Great), Quirinius a Roman senator, became governor (Legate) of Syria, while an equestrian assistant named Coponius was assigned as the first governor of the newly created Judaea Province. These governors were assigned to conduct a tax census for the Emperor in Syria and Judaea."

Joseph Ratzinzer (Pope Benedict XVI), in his book *The Infancy Narratives: Jesus of Nazareth,* p. 62 supports this view of a Census in 6 B.C. He does note, however, that there is much debate regarding the date of the census. Quoting Alois he states:

"Alois Stoger suggests that the 'population census' was a slow process in the conditions of the time, dragging on over several years. Moreover, it was implemented in two stages: firstly, registration of all land and property ownership, and then in the second phase - determination of the payments that were due. The first stage would have taken place at the time of Jesus' birth . . . " (Lukasevangelium, pp. 372 ff.),

The Star of Bethlehem: The New Evidence
John C. Iannone

According to this dating (6-7 B.C.), some historians say the Gospel of Luke reflects a date for Jesus' birth earlier than the years 3-2 B.C. and, therefore, not in line with the conjunctions of the star and planets we propose. However, there was another, later, census often overlooked by some historians.

An Alternative View on the Census:

Most modern scholars explain the disparity as an error on the part of the author of the Gospel, concluding that he was more concerned with creating a symbolic narrative than a historical account, and was either unaware of, or indifferent to, the chronological difficulty.

However, more contemporary research, as noted in John P. Pratt's article *"Yet Another Eclipse for Herod,"* points out that there was, in fact, an Empire-Wide Registration in 3/2 B.C. consistent with the Gospel of Luke:

> " . . . a combined census and oath of allegiance to Augustus Caesar in 3-2 B.C. perhaps related to the bestowal of the title '**pater patriae**' (**Father of Thy Country**) by the Roman Senate on February 5, 2 B.C." (Res Gestae 35; Ovid, Fasti 2, 129) The Planetarium, Vol. 19, No. 4, Dec. 1990, pp. 8-14).

Pratt cites Orosius (a fifth century historian) clearly linking an oath to the registration at the birth of Christ:

> "Augustus ordered that a census be taken of each province everywhere and that all men be enrolled. So at that time, Christ was born and was entered on the Roman census list as soon as he was born. This is the earliest and most famous public acknowledgment which market Caesar as the first of all men and the Romans as lords of the world . . . that first and greatest census was taken, since in this one name of Caesar all the peoples of the great nations took oath, and at the same time, through the participation in the census, were made part of one society. (Orosius, *Adv. Pag.* V1 22.7, V11.2.16 by Deferrari, R.J. *The Fathers of the Church* (Washington, D.C.: Catholic U. Press, 1964, Vol. 50, p. 281, 287).

Verse 3, 4, 5: Joseph and Mary go to Bethlehem:

Everyone went to their own town to register. **Joseph and Mary go to Bethlehem, the town of David** because Joseph belonged to the house and line of David. Remember that David was the first King of the Tribe of Judah from which the Messiah would come.

The Star of Bethlehem: The New Evidence
John C. Iannone

Note: Bethlehem, according to the **Prophet Micah** was the town from which the Savior would be born:

> *"But you, Bethlehem Ephrathah, though you are small among the clans of Judah, out of you will come for me one who will be ruler over Israel, whose origins are from of old, from ancient times."' (Micah 5:2)*

The beautiful Christmas Carol *"Lo, How a Rose ere Blooming"* talks of the Messiah coming from "Jesse's lineage." Jesse was the father of King David. The text is thought to be penned by an anonymous author, and the piece first appeared in print in the late 16th century. The hymn has been used by both Catholics and Protestants;

"Lo, how a Rose e'er blooming from tender stem hath sprung!

Of Jesse's lineage coming, as men of old have sung.

It came, a floweret bright, amid the cold of winter,

When half spent was the night.

Isaiah 'twas foretold it, the Rose I have in mind;

With Mary we behold it, the virgin mother kind.

To show God's love aright, she bore to men a Savior,

When half spent was the night."

Verses 6 and 7: Jesus was born in a Manger because there was no guest room available for them.

Note: **A manger** is a feeding trough found in a stable. In Biblical times   mangers were made from clay mixed with straw or from stones held together with mud sometimes they were carved in natural outcroppings of rock.

The Star of Bethlehem: The New Evidence
John C. Iannone

(Photograph at Megiddo where this manger (feeding trough) was used in the stables of King Ahab - Megiddo, Israel. Taken by David Padfield www.padfield.com).

Note: In line with the concept of a "manger" as a feeding trough found in a "stable," Christian author and speaker Nick Page has published a new book in which he explains that a **stable** was more of a guestroom located where the animals slept in the lower area of the home. In *Whatever happened to the Ark of the Covenant?* Page sets out to separate the Nativity facts from the myths.

> "The actual Greek word used by Luke does not refer to an inn at all, but to a guestroom. Most likely Mary and Joseph were lodging with relatives. There wasn't enough room, so they were sleeping in the place where the animals are kept."

> "In peasant households of the time, animals were kept in the lower part of the house, partly so the animals wouldn't be stolen, and partly because the heat from their bodies provided a kind of rudimentary central heating."

The earliest homes in Palestine at the time of Jesus did usually have a lower area for animals in a similar way that we have a garage alongside of or below our living areas for our automobiles. The animals of our ancestors were like our autos today, vital modes of transportation, and were kept separate from the living quarters.

Verse 8: Shepherds were keeping watch over their flocks by night.

We traditionally think of Christmas as December 25th, but this date is not consistent with the statement of Luke 2:8 that: *"there were shepherds living out in the fields nearby, keeping watch over their flocks at night."* In the early Church, the date of December 25th came to be the date associated with Christmas. For now, we seek to understand the meaning of *"shepherds living out in the fields."*

The Lambing Season:

The period of shepherds living out in the fields is often referred to as *the lambing season* and occurred in the spring/summer months.

"It is clear that the shepherds are living in the fields with their sheep. The Greek word translated here in the New American Standard Version as 'staying out' is *'agrauloúntes'.* It means that they were staying overnight; the shepherds were 'camping out', so to speak. In the King James Version, the expression translated as 'abiding in' the fields with their sheep. They are not out on a day trip, at least not according to the scripture. They are actually living out there with their flock! This certainly seems to indicate that we are within the range of time when shepherds drove their sheep into the open fields and stayed with them for the May to October time period. They are already out there at the time of Jesus' birth, and they apparently have not yet returned. If nothing else, this seems to indicate that Jesus is born sometime between May and October, and certainly not as late in the winter as December." www.pleaseconvinceme.com

In the following *Chart of Average Temperature in Israel,* note that the summer temperatures are consistent with the period of the Shepherds living in the fields (the lambing period).

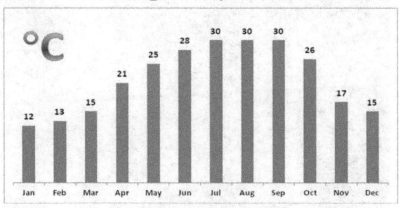

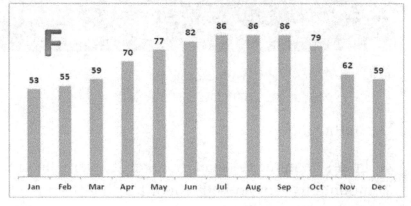

Courtesy: www.goisrael.com – Tourism

The Star of Bethlehem: The New Evidence
John C. Iannone

www.observadores-cometas.com/cometas/Star/Visibility_Star.htm

The author notes:

"Luke's comment that shepherds were in the mountains around Bethlehem tending their flocks by night is totally inconsistent with the Nativity having taken place in winter. The weather in Jerusalem, which is 6km north of Bethlehem and at similar altitude, is cool and humid between October and March; moderate frosts and heavy snowfall are by no means unknown. A comparison with shepherds that use traditional methods in the central plateau of Spain, where the altitude and climatic conditions are similar, suggests that night-time vigil is a feature of lambing time in spring and possibly of summer if there are large predators such as wolves in the region of the pastures."

Research will demonstrate that it was likely in the summer (June) of 2 B.C. that Jesus was born.

Verses 9 – 15: An Angel appears to them to announce that a Savior has been born to you; He is the Messiah, the Lord. The Shepherds go to Bethlehem and find Mary, Joseph and the baby. Jesus' name was given by the angel.

Distinguishing the Infant Baby from The Child Jesus:

Note that Luke refers to the "baby" Jesus. In Verses 12 and 16, Luke uses the Greek term βρέφος (brephos) in talking about the infant.

Verse 12 "This will be a sign to you: You will find a baby (βρέφος) wrapped in clothes and lying in a manger."

The Greek word used here for baby is βρέφος meaning "infant, baby, babe, suckling, nursling."

Verse 16: So they hurried off and found Mary and Joseph, and the baby (βρέφος) who was lying in the manger.

Verses 17 and 21: In these verses, Luke changes the name to παιδίον (Paidiou and Paidion), Greek meaning child. Matthew uses this phrase when talking about a slightly older Jesus visited by the Magi in Jesus' home in Bethlehem.

CHAPTER FIVE

THE STAR AND THE GOSPEL OF MATTHEW

"Hark! The herald angels sing,

Glory to the new born King,

Peace on earth, and mercy mild,

God and sinners reconciled!

Joyful, all ye nations rise,

Join the triumph of the skies;

With angelic host proclaim,

Christ is born in Bethlehem!

Hark! The herald angels sing,

Glory to the new born King!"

("Hark! The herald angels sing" is a popular Christmas Carol attributed to Charles Wesley, 1707-1788; alt. by George Whitefield and others).

www.crystalinks.com

The Gospel of Matthew: 2: 1-22

1. "After Jesus was born in Bethlehem in Judea, during the time of King Herod, Magi from the east came to Jerusalem

2 and asked, "Where is the one who has been born king of the Jews? We saw his star when it rose and have come to worship him."

3 When King Herod heard this he was disturbed, and all Jerusalem with him.

4 When he had called together all the people's chief priests and teachers of the law, he asked them where the Messiah was to be born.

5 "In Bethlehem in Judea," they replied, "for this is what the prophet has written:

6 "But you, Bethlehem, in the land of Judah, are by no means least among the rulers of Judah; for out of you will come a ruler who will shepherd my people Israel."' Micah 5: 2-4

7 Then Herod called the Magi secretly and found out from them the exact time the star had appeared.

8 He sent them to Bethlehem and said, "Go and search carefully for the child. As soon as you find him, report to me, so that I too may go and worship him."

9 After they had heard the king, they went on their way, and the star they had seen when it rose went ahead of them until it stopped over the place where the child was.

10 When they saw the star, they were overjoyed.

11 On coming to the house, they saw the child with his mother Mary, and they bowed down and worshiped him. Then they opened their treasures and presented him with gifts of gold, frankincense and myrrh.

12 And having been warned in a dream not to go back to Herod, they returned to their country by another route.

The Escape to Egypt

13 When they had gone, an angel of the Lord appeared to Joseph in a dream. "Get up," he said, "take the child and his mother and escape to Egypt. Stay there until I tell you, for Herod is going to search for the child to kill him."

14 So he got up, took the child and his mother during the night and left for Egypt,

15 where he stayed until the death of Herod. And so was fulfilled what the Lord had said through the prophet: "Out of Egypt I called my son." (Hosea 11:1).

16 When Herod realized that he had been outwitted by the Magi, he was furious, and he gave orders to kill all the boys in Bethlehem and its vicinity who were two years old and under, in accordance with the time he had learned from the Magi.

17 Then what was said through the prophet Jeremiah was fulfilled:

18 "A voice is heard in Ramah, weeping and great mourning, Rachel weeping for her children and refusing to be comforted, because they are no more." (Jeremiah 31:15)

The Return to Nazareth

19 After Herod died, an angel of the Lord appeared in a dream to Joseph in Egypt

20 and said, "Get up, take the child and his mother and go to the land of Israel, for those who were trying to take the child's life are dead."

21 So he got up, took the child and his mother and went to the land of Israel.

22 But when he heard that Archelaus was reigning in Judea in place of his father Herod, he was afraid to go there. Having been warned in a dream, he withdrew to the district of Galilee,

23 and he went and lived in a town called Nazareth. So was fulfilled what was said through the prophets, that he would be called a Nazarene."

Some Notes on the Versus of Matthew:

Verse 1: Jesus was born in Bethlehem during the time of King Herod and Magi came from the east.

Note: This was Herod the Great, not his son Herod Antipas.

> "Herod was the pro-Roman king of the small Jewish state in the last decades before the Common Era. He started his career as a general, but the Roman statesman Mark Antony recognized him as the Jewish national leader. During a war against the Parthians, Herod was removed from the scene, but the Roman Senate made him king and gave him soldiers to seize the throne. As 'friend and ally of the Romans' he was not a truly independent king; however, Rome allowed him a domestic policy of his own. Although Herod tried to respect the pious feeling of his subjects, many of them were not content with his rule, which ended in terror. He was succeeded by his sons." www.livius.org

Matthew notes that the Magi came from the east. I will mention here what Matthew DOESN'T say but which has grown in tradition.

a. He doesn't say they were Kings, only that they were wise men from the East. We infer they were kings from the Psalms.

b. He doesn't say there were three of them. There were likely more. We infer that there were three from the fact that they brought gold, frankincense and myrrh – 3 gifts.

Barry Setterfield in his **DVD** *"The Christmas Star: Do Astronomy and History Support The Bible?"* **says** it was a large contingent of Parthians that entered Jerusalem. However, I am not convinced this was the case. The Magi were likely Babylonians (from modern Iraq). The Romans and Parthians (Persians from what is not modern Iran) were mortal enemies and it is unlikely that the Romans or King Herod would allow a virtual "army" of Persians to enter Roman territory unchallenged. I do believe, as Setterfield suggests, that it was a meaningful retinue supporting the Magi. Western tradition holds there were three Magi while Eastern Christians believe there were twelve plus those that served them.

c. Matthew doesn't say they went to the stable/manger. He states that they went the "*house*" (οἰκίαν) of Mary and saw the "*child*" – Greek "**paidon**" meaning a child or toddler.

Verse 2: "We saw his star when it rose. . .."

This is the first mention of a Star. Matthew is the only Gospel that speaks of the Magi and the Star.

Verses 3 and 4: Herod is disturbed. He calls the Chief Priests and Teachers together and asks where the Messiah is to be born.

Verses 5 and 6: They quote the Prophet Micah who said the child would be born in Bethlehem.

Verses 7 and 8: Herod calls the Magi and wants them to tell him where they find the child so he could worship him.

Verse 9: *"and the star they had seen when it rose went ahead of them until it stopped over the place where the child was.*

Note: Reference to the phrase that the star "stopped over the place" refers to the fact that Jupiter was in retrograde and would appear to stop relative to the motion of the Earth. Retrograde will be discuss in Chapter 11.

Note: The use of the term "child" as opposed to the infant Jesus suggests He is not the infant in the manger but a child. Luke uses the term child παιδίον to mean a **toddler**, around 1 to 2 years old.

> Note: Collins English Dictionary – Complete and Unabridged © HarperCollins Publishers 1991, 1994, 1998, 2000, and 2003 defines a toddler as "a young child, usually between the ages of one and two and a half."

Verse 11: *"On coming to the house, they saw the child with his mother Mary, and they bowed down and worshiped him."*

As noted above, Luke uses the term "house" as opposed to a stable or manger. Jesus is now a young child, a toddler, in a home when the Magi visit Him.

> The New American Standard Hebrew-Aramaic and Greek dictionaries state that παιδίον (**paidion**) is a young child:

Verse 16: "When Herod realized that he had been outwitted by the Magi, he was furious, and he gave orders to kill all the boys in Bethlehem and its vicinity who were two years old and under. . ."

Note: This supports Matthew's meaning that *paidion* was used for children after they were approximately 1 -

2 years old, likely a toddler. The fact that we are dealing with a "child" in a "home" and that Herod orders the killing of boys two years and under indicates that the Magi visited Jesus when he was between one and two years of age. This is important for helping to determine the time of Jesus' birth.

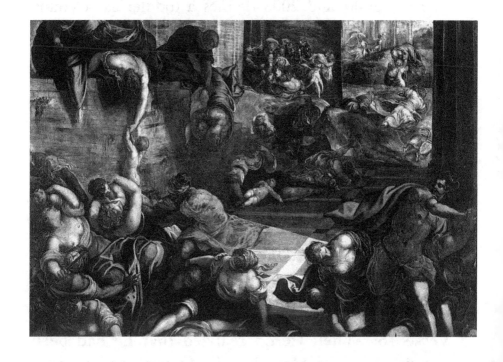

Slaughter of the Innocents by Tintoretto. Style: High Renaissance. Lived: 1518 - 1594 (16th century)

www.artinthepicture.com/paintings/Tintoretto/The-Slaughter-of-the-Innocents

CHAPTER SIX

SEEKING THE DATE WHEN WAS JESUS BORN

"Silent night, holy night

All is calm, all is bright

Round yon Virgin, Mother and Child

Holy Infant so tender and mild

Sleep in heavenly peace

Sleep in heavenly peace

Silent night, holy night!

Shepherds quake at the sight

Glories stream from heaven afar

Heavenly hosts sing Alleluia!

Christ, the Saviour is born

Christ, the Saviour is born

Silent night, holy night

Son of God, love's pure light

Radiant beams from Thy holy face

With the dawn of redeeming grace

Jesus, Lord, at Thy birth

Jesus, Lord, at Thy birth "

(Silent Night" (German: Stille Nacht, heilige Nacht) is a popular Christmas carol, composed in 1818 by Franz Xaver Gruber to lyrics by Joseph Mohr in the small town of Oberndorf bei Salzburg, Austria). www.en.wikipedia.org

----

Dating the Death of Herod the Great:

When did King Herod the great die? In our efforts to determine the date of Jesus' birth and how it correlates with celestial events indicating the Star of Bethlehem, it is important to determine the correct year of the death of Herod the Great since Jesus was obviously born during his reign and since He was approximately one to two years old when Herod slaughtered the innocents.

(Note: There is no actual evidence that Herod killed the babies of Bethlehem, outside of the Gospel of Matthew. However, given Herod's propensity for killing, it is likely true. It is estimated that there may have been only 1,500 to 2,000 people living in Bethlehem and the number of babies under two is estimated at about 20, half being female. The number is small and, given Herod's other slaughters, may have seemed insignificant to extra-biblical writers such as Josephus at the time).

Many authors have indicated that Josephus, the Jewish historian writing around 90 A.D., indicated that Herod the Great died in 4 B.C. Since Jesus was born during the reign of King Herod, he would have been around 1 to 2 years old when Herod died, making Jesus' birth around 5 to 6 B.C. (if Herod's death was, in fact, 4 B.C.)

However, several historians believe that Josephus was misinterpreted and that he was indicating that Herod died most likely in early 1 A.D. making the birth of Jesus around 3 to 2 B.C.

The Jewish Lunar Calendar:

The Romans kept a **solar calendar**, as we do today, with the exception that Greeks and Romans, following Aristotle and Ptolemy, believed the Sun moved around the Earth and that the Earth was the center of the universe. The Jews, however, kept a **lunar calendar**, basing their dates on the phases and eclipses of the moon. Josephus was a Jew and often recorded events based on lunar phases and eclipses. Key to our thesis is that, while many historians assumed that Herod died in 4 B.C., Josephus never says that "Herod died in 4 B.C." It is this assumption by several historians that has now been challenged..

What Did Josephus Actually Say?

Josephus says, in *Antiquities Book 17 Chapter 6 Paragraph 4*, that Herod died after a lunar eclipse:

> *"And that very night there was an eclipse of the moon."* (referring to the night when a high priest was killed by Herod due to an insurrection involving removal of a golden eagle from the Temple Gate).

> (Taken from *The Complete Works of Josephus* translated by Wm. Whiston., Kregel Publications, Grand Rapids, MI, 1981).

Whiston, the translator, then adds a critical footnote, one that has led future writers to interpret this as the lunar eclipse of 4 B.C.

"This eclipse of the moon (which is the only eclipse mentioned by Josephus) is of the greatest consequence for the determination of the time for the death of Herod ..., and for the birth and entire chronology of Jesus Christ. It happened March 13th, in the year of the Julian period 4710 and the 4th year before the Christian era."

Unfortunately, up until recent times, scholars tended to accept Whiston's theory without question. However, new evidence has emerged indicating that Josephus was, in fact, likely referring to a later total eclipse that occurred in on December 29, 1 B.C. and that the eclipse of March 13, 4 B.C. was NOT the only eclipse of Herod's reign.

Whiston's statement is a misleading argument because if Whiston assumes that Herod died in 4 B.C. and mentions an eclipse which he says is "the only eclipse mentioned by Josephus," he assumes Josephus must be talking of this eclipse in 4 B.C.

The Total Lunar Eclipses of January 10, 1 B.C. and December 29, 1 B.C.

There were, however, TWO eclipses of the moon later in Herod's reign: one on January 9-10, 1 B.C., and one on December 29, 1 B.C. It is this second eclipse of December 29, 1 B.C. which is believed by many modern scholars to be the eclipse that Josephus is referring to, making Herod's death in 1 A.D. a few months later and making this a <u>third</u> eclipse during the latter part of Herod's reign.

In their work, *"Solar and Lunar Eclipses of the Ancient Near East",* by M. Kudlek and E. Mickler (1971) they mention;

"Lunar Eclipses Visible in Palestine:

7 B.C. No eclipses

6 B.C. No eclipses

5 B.C. March 23. Total eclipse. Central at 8:30 pm (elapsed time between eclipse and Passover: twenty-nine days).

5 B.C. September 15. Total eclipse. Central at 10:30 pm (elapsed time between eclipse and Passover: seven months).

4 B.C. March 13. Partial eclipse. Central at 2:20 am (elapsed time between eclipse and Passover: twenty-nine days).

> Note: this is the eclipse referred to by Whiston. It does not fit the history because the short period of 29 days between the eclipse of March 13, 4 B.C. and Passover April 11, 4 B.C. does not allow

sufficient time for the many events recorded by Josephus between the partial eclipse and Passover.

3 B.C. No eclipses

2 B.C. No eclipses

1 B.C. January 10. Total eclipse. Central at 1:00 am (elapsed time between eclipse and Passover: twelve and a half weeks).

1 B.C. December 29. A second total eclipse and likely the one referred to by Josephus.

Why December 29, 1 B.C. Eclipse vs. January 9-10 Eclipse?

Astronomer John Pratt makes a case for the Dec. 29, 1 B.C.:

" . . . the eclipses of March 13, 4 B.C. and January 10, 1 B.C. are extremely unlikely because they both began the umbral phase more than six hours after sunset and hence would have only been seen by at most a few people. The eclipse of Sept. 15, 5 B.C. began three hours after sunset, but that is also late. On the other hand, the eclipse of December 29, 1 B.C. fits this criterion very well. The full moon was nearly half eclipsed when it could first be seen rising in the east above the distant mountains about twenty minutes after sunset . . . Of the candidates to be Herod's eclipse, the December 29, 1 B.C. eclipse was the most likely to have been widely observed." (Pratt, *Yet Another Eclipse for Herod*, The Planetarium, Vol. 19, no. 4, Dec. 1990, pp. 8-14).

Since Josephus mentioned a number of events that transpired between the eclipse of March 13, 4 B.C. and the Passover 29 days later on April 11, 4 B.C. (excluding the days of the 13th March and 11th April) many authors have noted that it was <u>virtually impossible for all the events mentioned by Josephus to take place during this period</u>, and therefore that Josephus was NOT talking about the eclipse of 4 B.C. but that he was talking of the Total Eclipse on December 29, 1 B.C.

What Were The Events That Took Place?

The publication of Ernest Martin's *The Birth of Christ* in 1978 acknowledged the difficulties with the 4 B.C. date for the death of Herod. Juan Antonio Revilla, elaborating on Martin's statements, tells us in his article *"On The Year of Herod's Death"* that:

> "Josephus mentions that Herod died in the interval between a Lunar eclipse and the following Passover. For centuries this has been thought to be the eclipse of **March 13, 4 B.C.**

and that the evidence of astronomy has been decisive to establish the dogma that Herod died that year."

"Recent calculations, however, showed that this eclipse was only partial, and that the events narrated by Josephus to have occurred between this eclipse and the Passover that followed are impossible if one takes the 4 B.C. date, while the total eclipses of **January 9-10, 1 B.C. and 29 December, 1 B.C. eliminate those problems.**"

Revilla maintains that the one on 29 December, 1 B.C. was:

"the most likely candidate because it happened in the evening and would have been observed by many people."

Revilla's argument, based on Martin's work, states that proponents of the theory that Herod died in 4 B.C. postulate that the following events all happened within 29 days from the partial eclipse to the Passover (which is highly unlikely):

Events mentioned by Josephus after the Eclipse of 4 B.C.:

... "Herod's sickness increases and part of Herod's body was putrefied and bred worms."

The Star of Bethlehem: The New Evidence
John C. Iannone

. . . He took trips to the warm sulfuric baths across the Jordan at Callirrhoe, returning when treatment failed. (Josephus XVII, Chapter VI, Sec. V). These trips to the northeast side of the Dead Sea took time.

. . . Herod orders that all important men in all villages up to 70-80 miles away to come to Jerusalem where they were imprisoned at the Hippodrome to be killed at the time of Herod's death. This would ensure, in Herod's distorted mind, that all Palestine would mourn his death. Communication with all the villages plus the preparations and trip required by each man took time. The Leaders were later released after Herod's death.

. . . His son Antipator is executed and Herod dies 5 days later.

. . . There is a magnificent funeral which required substantial planning. The body is carried from Jericho, where he died, to Herodium south of Jerusalem with great fanfare. Josephus says:

> "About the bier were his sons and numerous relations; next was the soldiery distinguished according to their several countries and denominations in the following order: First of all went his guards; then the band of Thracians; and after them the Germans; and next the band of Galatians, everyone in their habiliments of war;

and behind these marched the whole army in the same manner as they used to go out to war . . . these were followed by five hundred of his domestics, carrying spices. So they went eight furlongs to Herodium; for there, by his own command, he was to be buried: and thus did Herod end his life. *(Josephus XVII, Chapter VIII, Section 3).*

Note: In his *Jewish Wars*, Josephus says it was 200 stadia (or approximately 23 miles from Jericho to Herodium). The mention of 8 furlongs in *Antiquities* was likely the distance outside the city of Herodium where the tomb was located).

This elaborate funeral took substantial time and planning. Pratt notes that carrying the body on a bier by hand for long distances was not uncommon. By comparison, the body of Augustus was carried 120 miles by dignitaries (A.D. 14). Tiberius walked all the way from Germany to Rome with the body of his brother in 9 B.C." (Suetonius, *Augustus C.2*; Tiberius V11.3)."

. . . A 7-day mourning began followed by a funeral feast.

. . . Another public mourning was planned for the patriots who had been executed during the day preceding the night of the eclipse."

Martin maintains that it was impossible for all these events to happen in less than 54 days (not the 29 days from the lunar eclipsed of 4 B.C. to the Passover).

The Marble Steps to Herod's Tomb Found:

In a *London Times* story in May 2007, Professor Ehud Netzer of Hebrew University in Jerusalem announced to the world that, after a lifetime search, he located and uncovered the remains of Herod the Great's tomb in Herodium. The body was not there, likely stolen. Herodium is a man-made fortress of immense scale with many buildings, monuments, track ways and open spaces about 8 miles south of Jerusalem and just to the south of Bethlehem.

Interestingly, Prof. Netzer indicated it was an ancient staircase built for Herod's funeral processions, described by Josephus, that led Prof. Netzer's team to the hill-top burial site. Prof. Netzer indicates "The monumental stairs were built specifically for the funeral." (www.new.bbc.co.uk)

Josephus stated:

> "Two hundred steps of purest white marble led up to it (Herod's tomb). Its top was crowned with circular towers; its courtyard contained splendid structures."

It would appear highly unlikely that, in the short time from the March 13, 4 B.C. lunar eclipse and the April 11, 4 B.C. Passover, builders could have quarried, carved, transported and placed "two hundred steps of purest white marble" specifically for the funeral.

(Location of Herodium south of Jerusalem. Herod's body was carried from Jericho (about 15 miles northeast of Jerusalem) to Herodium (approximately 23 miles from Jericho and just south of Bethlehem).

Herod's Tomb.   www.smithsonianmag.com

The Star of Bethlehem: The New Evidence
John C. Iannone

(Herod, also known as Herod the Great and Herod I, was a Roman client king of Judea. He is described as "a madman who murdered his own family and a great many rabbis." He was the father of Herod Antipas, Herod Archelaus, Philip the Tetrarch, and builder of the Great Temple of Jerusalem")

The Star of Bethlehem: The New Evidence
John C. Iannone

(The Great Temple in Jerusalem during the time of Jesus).

In his book *The Star of Bethlehem, The Star that Astonished the World*, Professor Ernest L. Martin (Chapter 8) states:

> "They particularly preferred this eclipse (December 29, 1 B.C.) because Josephus also said Herod died before a springtime Passover. Since March 13, 4 B.C.E. was just one month before the Passover; they felt justified in placing all historical events associated with Herod's death and his funeral within that twenty-nine day period. The truth is, however, it is completely

illogical to squeeze the events mentioned by Josephus into that short period of time. By selecting the wrong eclipse, modern scholars have been forced to tighten considerably the historical events into an abnormally compressed space of only twenty-nine days."

He continues:

"With the eclipse of Josephus, none of these factors is evident. Josephus gave the single clue that a springtime Passover was celebrated not long after the eclipse. This would appear a reasonable hint that the eclipse happened sometime in the early or late winter. It is the mention of this Passover that prompted most theologians up to now to select the eclipse of March 13, 4 B.C.E. as the one that seems to meet the historical circumstances. But this is not possible. A close examination of the records provided by Josephus unearths formidable problems in accepting this eclipse. Using common sense, plus the application of a general understanding of the Jewish social and religious customs in the 1st century, will allow anyone to select the proper eclipse. In no way can it be the one of March 13, 4 B.C.E."

Herod's death in early 1 A.D. is much more supportive of Josephus' statement and supportive of Jesus' conception and birth in 3 B.C. - 2 B.C.

Early Church Fathers on the Date of Jesus' Birth:

Testimony supporting the year of Jesus' birth as 3/2BC is found in the writings of the early Church Fathers. In approximately the year 200AD, **St. Clement of Alexandria**, head of the Christian catechetical school in Alexandria, Egypt, is supportive of 3/2 B.C:

Finegan's *Handbook of Biblical Chronology* shows a Table reflecting that, among others, these Fathers of the Church attributed the birth of Jesus as follows: (all dates are B.C.).

Cesiodorus Senator – 3 B.C.

Clement of Alexandria – 3/2

Tertullian – 3/2

Origen – 3/2

Hippolytus of Rome – 3/2

Hippolytus of Thebes (1st fragment) – 3/2

Eusebius – 3/2

The Star of Bethlehem: The New Evidence
John C. Iannone

(See also: Juan Antonio Revilla, *"On The Year of Herod's Death"* referring to David Hughes book on *The Star of Bethlehem,*(1980, p. 94).

New Testament Chronology Supportive of 2 B.C :

The New Testament texts provide clues as to the year of the birth of Jesus, likely in 2 B.C.

In Luke 13:23 we read:

> "Now Jesus himself was about thirty years old when he began his ministry.."

In Luke 3: 1-2:

> "In the fifteenth year of Tiberius Caesar's reign, when Pontius Pilate was governor of Judaea, Herod tetrarch of Galilee, his brother Philip tetrarch of the territories of Ituraea and Trachonitis, Lysanias tetrarch of Abilene, and while the high-priesthood was held by Annas and Caiaphas, the word of God came to John (the Baptist) the son of Zechariah, in the desert."

The Roman Emperor Tiberius succeeded his step-father, Augustus Caesar, on the 19th of August in 14 AD. Therefore, the 15th year of Tiberius' reign, when St. John the Baptist and Jesus began their ministries (as the Romans calculated their years) was 28 AD. Subtracting thirty years from 28 A.D.. would bring Jesus' birth to 2 B.C.

That both the priest St. John the Baptist and Jesus, the rightful Davidic king, were thirty years old when they began their ministries, is significant.

A priest began his full ministerial duties when he was thirty and King David began to rule over Israel when he was thirty years old (Numbers 4:34-35; 2 Samuel 5:4). This is also information that is useful in calculating Jesus' birth.

St. Luke provided the information that the Angel Gabriel indicated that St. John the Baptist was six months older than Jesus:

> Luke 1: 36-37: "And I tell you this too: your cousin Elizabeth also, in her old age, has conceived a son, and she whom people called barren is now in her sixth month."

From the year calculated as the beginning of St. John the Baptist's ministry and the information concerning the difference in months between John and Jesus' conceptions, it can be calculated that both St. John and Jesus' births were likely in the year 2 B.C..

The Star of Bethlehem: The New Evidence
John C. Iannone

Dionysius Exiguus and the Anno Domini A.D.

"Dionysius Exiguus, is a celebrated 6th-century Scythian monk and scholar. He is generally considered the inventor of the Christian calendar (**A.D. is Anno Domino – the Year of Our Lord**), the use of which spread through the employment of his new Easter tables.

The 6th-century historian Cassiodorus calls him a monk who arrived in Rome about the time of the death (496 A.D.) of Pope St. Gelasius I, who had summoned him to organize the pontifical archives. Thereafter, Dionysius flourished as a scholar at Rome. In 525 A.D., at the request of Pope St. John I, he prepared the chronology still current for the **Anno Domini**. According to some, he wrongly dated the birth of Christ as December 25, 1 B.C. according to the Roman system (i.e., 754 years after the founding of Rome) as Dec. 25, 753.

The Star of Bethlehem: The New Evidence
John C. Iannone

http://www.britannica.com/EBchecked/topic/164239/DionysiusExiguus

Was Dionysius Wrong?

Dionysius is frequently stated in literature to have been wrong about his dating of the birth of Jesus which he says was on or near December 25, 1 B.C. Those that say he is incorrect maintain that the death of Herod was 4 B.C., as just discussed, and Jesus was about 1 to 2 years old, making His birth – according to Dionysius' critics – about 5/6 B.C. However, the dating of Herod's death just after the total lunar eclipse of Dec. 29, 1 B.C. makes Dionysius much closer to the correct dating that we maintain is June 2 B.C. Note: we already indicated that Luke's Gospel has the shepherds living in the fields when the angels appear to them. Shepherds lived in the fields during the spring/summer months – the lambing period – making June a much more likely candidate than December.

As previously noted by John P. Pratt,

> "Many conjunctions in the 3-2 B.C. skies have been noted that might have been interpreted by the Magi as being signs of the birth of Christ, but one far excels the others as being truly outstanding. The conjunction of Jupiter and Venus on June 17, 2 B.C. was so close that the two planets would have appeared to touch each

other. Calculations indicate that there has never been a brighter, closer conjunction of Venus and Jupiter so near to the bright star Regulus in Leo in the 2000 years before or since." John P. Pratt: *"Yet Another Eclipse for Herod,"* The Planetarium, Vol. 19, No. 4, Dec. 1990, pp. 8-14.

Conclusion:

The most logical conclusion is that it is more likely that Herod died in 1 A.D. a few months after the total lunar eclipse of December 29, 1 B.C. Jesus was a toddler at this time (Herod ordered the slaughter of the children 2 years and younger expecting Jesus to be in this group). This would fit with Him being born likely in 2 B.C.

CHAPTER SEVEN

THE TOWN OF BETHLEHEM

"O little town of Bethlehem

How still we see thee lie

Above thy deep and dreamless sleep

The silent stars go by

Yet in thy dark streets shineth

The everlasting Light

The hopes and fears of all the years

Are met in thee tonight

For Christ is born of Mary

And gathered all above

While mortals sleep, the angels keep

Their watch of wondering love

O morning stars together

Proclaim the holy birth

And praises sing to God the King

And Peace to men on earth."

(Written by Phillips Brooks in 1865, an Episcopal priest, Rector of the Church of the Holy Trinity, Philadelphia after visiting Bethlehem in 1865).

Rich Bassett:
http://thecornfedpastor.wordpress.com/2011/12/22/o-little-town-of-bethlehem

The Prophesy of Micah:

Micah, meaning "who is like the Lord?" was a prophet from approximately 737-696 B.C. in Judah and is the author of the Book of Micah.

The Prophet Micah.

Courtesy *www.theomegadays.net*.

He is best known for his prophesy regarding the location of Jesus' birth in Bethlehem of Judea:

"But you, Bethlehem Ephrathah,

though you are small among the clans of Judah,

out of you will come for me

one who will be ruler over Israel,

whose origins are from of old,

from ancient times." Micah 5:2

What do we know of Bethlehem?

Bethlehem is the town in which Mary bore the baby Jesus. In an article by Mary Fairchild, we learn the following:

> "The city of Bethlehem, located about six miles south of Jerusalem, means 'house of bread.' Bethlehem was also the renowned City of David. It was there in young David's hometown that the prophet Samuel anointed him to be king over Israel." (Mary Fairchild, www.About.com - Christianity)

Bethlehem in the Old Testament:

In the Old Testament, Bethlehem was an early Canaanite settlement connected with the patriarchs. Situated along an ancient caravan route, Bethlehem has harbored a melting pot of peoples and cultures since its beginning. The geography of the region is mountainous, sitting about 2,600 feet above the Mediterranean Sea.

King David was born and raised in Bethlehem. Bethlehem eventually came to be called the City of David as the symbol of his great dynasty, and it grew into an important, strategic, and fortified city.

In addition, Bethlehem is noted in connection with the Babylonian Exile (Jeremiah 41:17, Ezra 2:21), as some of the Jews returning from captivity stayed near Bethlehem on their way to Egypt.

Bethlehem in the New Testament

By the time of Jesus' birth, Bethlehem had declined in significance to a small village. Three gospel accounts (Matthew 2:1-12, Luke 2:4-20, and John 7:42) report that Jesus was born in the humble town of Bethlehem.

> **John 7: 42** *"Does not Scripture say that the Messiah will come from David's descendants and from Bethlehem, the town where David lived?"*

In summary, around the time Mary was due to give birth, Caesar Augustus decreed that a census be taken. Every person in the entire Roman world had to go to his own town to register. Joseph, being of the line of David, was required to go to Bethlehem to register with Mary. While in Bethlehem, Mary gave birth to Jesus.

The Star of Bethlehem: The New Evidence
John C. Iannone

Most likely due to the census, the inn was too crowded, and Mary gave birth to Jesus, placing Him in a Manger.

First shepherds and later wise men came to Bethlehem to worship the Christ-child. King Herod, who was ruler in Judea, plotted to kill the baby-king, ordering the slaughter of all male children two years old and younger in Bethlehem and surrounding areas.

In Matthew 2:16–18, we learned that Herod was furious when he realized that the wise men had outwitted him. He sent soldiers to kill all the boys in and around Bethlehem who were two years old and under, based on the wise men's report of the star's first appearance. Herod's brutal action fulfilled what God had spoken through the prophet Jeremiah: "A cry was heard in Ramah—weeping and great mourning. Rachel weeps for her children, refusing to be comforted, for they are dead." (NLT)

Present Day Bethlehem

Today, approximately 60,000 people live in and around the broader Bethlehem area. The population is divided primarily between Jews, Muslims and Christians, the Christians being predominately Orthodox.

"Under control of the Palestinian National Authority since 1995, Bethlehem city has experienced chaotic growth and a constant flow of tourism. It is home to one of the most sacred Christian sites in the world. Built by Constantine the Great (circa 330 A.D.), the **Church of the Nativity** still stands over a cave believed to be the very spot where Jesus was born. The place of the manger is marked by a 14-pointed silver star, called the star of Bethlehem."

"The original Church of the Nativity structure was partially destroyed by the Samaritans in 529 A.D. and then rebuilt by the Byzantine Roman emperor Justinian. It is one of the oldest surviving Christian churches in existence today." Mary Fairchild: *The Star of Bethlehem* (www.About.com - Christianity

Church of the Nativity: Bethlehem

Courtesy www.smithsonianmag.com

Interior of the Church of the Nativity: Bethlehem

Courtesy www.smithsonianmag.com

CHAPTER EIGHT

WHO WERE THE MAGI?

"We three kings of Orient are

Bearing gifts we traverse afar.

Field and fountain, moor and mountain,

Following yonder star.

O star of wonder, star of night,

Star with royal beauty bright,

Westward leading, still proceeding,

Guide us to thy perfect Light."

(Christmas carol written by the Episcopal Reverend John Henry Hopkins, Jr., who wrote both the lyrics and the music in 1857).

Courtesy www.fortheloveofhistruth.com

The Gospel of Matthew is the only one of the four Gospels to mention the Magi, or the Greek **"Magoi"** saying:

Matthew 2:1-2:

1. "After Jesus was born in Bethlehem in Judea, during the time of King Herod, Magi from the east came to Jerusalem

> *2. and asked, 'Where is the one who has been born king of the Jews? We saw his star when it rose and have come to worship him.' "*

Matthew does not say there were three Kings or Wise men, but does say they brought three gifts of gold, frankincense and myrrh so it is usually interpreted as three men.

Further, he does not even say that they were Kings. It was likely inferred from various Old Testament passages. In the Psalms and Isaiah we read:

> *Psalm 72:11: "May all kings bow down to him and all nations serve him."*

> *Isaiah 60: 3: "Nations will come to your light, and kings to the brightness of your dawn.*

> *Isaiah 68:29: "Because of your temple at Jerusalem, kings will bring you gifts."*

The word **magi** is the plural of the Latin *magus* borrowed from the Greek *magos* (μάγος) as used in the original Greek text of the Gospel of Matthew." The Greek *magos* is derived from Old Persian *magus*, the religious cast into which Zoroaster was born. The term refers originally to the priestly case of Zoroastrianism consisting of priests who paid particular attention to the stars and astrology, regarded at that time as a science. It was also applied to the Babylonian "wise men." The English term "magic" likely derived from the Magi.

Paul Maier, Professor of Ancient History at Western Michigan University, calls them "walking universities" steeped in the knowledge of the times, especially astronomy/astrology. He indicates that, being from a non-Jewish culture, the Magi added a "cross cultural" dimension to the coming of Jesus.

Viennese astronomer Konradin Ferrari d'Occhieppo adds an historical note about the existence of the Magi by stating that in the city of Babylon, which had once been a center of scientific astronomy but was already in decline by the time of Jesus, there was still:

> "a small group of astronomers who were gradually dying out . . . Earthenware tablets, covered in cuneiform signs with astronomical calculations . . . are clear proof of this." (*Der Stern von Bethlehem*, p. 27.). (Quoted by Joseph Ratzinger (Pope Emeritus Benedict XVI), in his book *The Infancy Narratives: Jesus of Nazareth*, p. 94).

Konradin Ferrari d'Occhieppo makes a further statement that:

> "the conjunction of the planets Jupiter and Saturn in the constellation of Pisces in the years 7-6 B.C. - now believed to be the actual time of Jesus' birth - is something that the Babylonian astronomers could have calculated."

Note: we will dispute further on Konradin's theory of Jupiter and Saturn in Pisces in 7-6 B.C. and build the case for Jupiter (the King Planet) and Venus (the Mother Planet) near Regulus (the King Star) in the Constellation of Leo, the Lion as the most likely conjunction at the time of the birth in June 2 B.C. (the Nativity).

The Prophet Daniel and the Magi:

How would the Babylonians become familiar with the traditions and beliefs of the Jews that Israel would someday see a Messiah, a King, and this would be written in the stars? How did they know the significance of the stars and heavens as they related to Jewish prophecy of the coming of a Messiah?

It is likely they learned this from the Prophet Daniel during the Babylonian Captivity (approx.. 597 BCE until the fall of Babylon to the Persian king Cyrus the Great in 538 BCE, who allowed the Jews to return to their homeland.

We learn that Daniel, captured during the Babylonian Captivity, was known and liked by the King of Babylon.

(Daniel in the Court of King Nebuchadnezzar, King of the Babylonian empire).

Courtesy www.chistianitymalaysia.com

Daniel 2: 48

> *"Then the king placed Daniel in a high position and lavished many gifts on him. He made him ruler over the entire province of Babylon and placed him in charge of all its wise men."*

The Star of Bethlehem: The New Evidence
John C. Iannone

Daniel, a devout Jew, and prisoner in Babylon won favor with the King of Babylon. Daniel brought with him a deep knowledge of the history of Israel and likely taught the Babylonian priests or Magi the scriptures about the Messiah and the Star.

Some excerpts from *The Book of the Prophet Daniel* may help to explain how the Magi became familiar with the prophesies of Israel regarding a Messiah and Star.

The book of Daniel was written by Daniel in 537 B.C.

Gordon states:

> "Daniel identifies himself as the author of the book in Daniel 12:4 and Jesus also identified him in Matt 24:15. Daniel was led into exile as a youth in 605 B.C. There he lived until the third year of Cyrus in 536 B.C. But how did Daniel, a Jewish boy, find himself exiled in Babylon? . . . Daniel's life is one of complete abandonment and devotion to the God of Israel."

The Babylonian Captivity:

Dan 1:1-2

"In the third year of the reign of Jehoiakim king of Judah, Nebuchadnezzar king of Babylon came to Jerusalem and besieged it. And the Lord delivered

Jehoiakim king of Judah into his hand, along with some of the articles from the temple of God. These he carried off to the temple of his god in Babylonia and put in the treasure house of his god."

Daniel, having been captured along with his fellow Jews, is introduced to the King's Court:

Dan 1:3-7

"Then the king ordered Ashpenaz, chief of his court officials, to bring in some of the Israelites from the royal family and the nobility— young men without any physical defect, handsome, showing aptitude for every kind of learning, well informed, quick to understand, and qualified to serve in the king's palace. He was to teach them the language and literature of the Babylonians. The king assigned them a daily amount of food and wine from the king's table. They were to be trained for three years, and after that they were to enter the king's service. Among these were some from Judah: Daniel, Hananiah, Mishael and Azariah."

Daniel learns the ways of the Babylonians but the student also teaches the master. He remains loyal to the ways of his God of Israel.

The Star of Bethlehem: The New Evidence
John C. Iannone

Dan 1:17-21 "

> *To these four young men God gave knowledge and understanding of all kinds of literature and learning. And Daniel could understand visions and dreams of all kinds. At the end of the time set by the king to bring them in, the chief official presented them to Nebuchadnezzar. The king talked with them, and he found none equal to Daniel, Hananiah, Mishael and Azariah; so they entered the king's service. In every matter of wisdom and understanding about which the king questioned them, he found them ten times better than all the magicians and enchanters in his whole kingdom. And Daniel remained there until the first year of King Cyrus.* "

It is likely from this text that Daniel brought knowledge of the history and way of Judaism including the Messianic prophesies and the star and imparted that to the wise men or magi of the Babylonians.

Daniel 2: 48:

> "He (the King) made him (Daniel) ruler over the entire province of Babylon and _placed him in charge of all its wise men._"

What were the names of the Wise Men who came to Bethlehem?

The Star of Bethlehem: The New Evidence
John C. Iannone

In the Western Christian Church they are known as: **Melchior, Caspar and Balthasar**, although, as previously noted, Matthew never said there were only three wise men, nor does the New Testament give any indication of their names.

According to Eastern Church tradition, Balthasar is often represented as a King of Arabia; Melchior as a King of Persia and Gaspar as a King of India." (The Encyclopedia Britannica).

Where did the Magi originate?

Matthew says only that they are *from the east,* more literally *from the rising (of the sun).* Traditionally, the view developed that they were Babylonians, Persians or even Jews from Yemen.

These Magi found Jesus by following a star (or conjunction of star and planets which appeared as one star), traditionally known as the Star of Bethlehem.

A Model for the Magi Journey?

"A model for the homage of the Magi might have been provided by the journey to Rome of King Tiridates I or Armenia with his magi, to pay homage to the Emperor Nero, which took place in 66 A.D. a few years before the date assigned to the composition of the Gospel of Matthew." www.en.wikipedia.org quoting from ^ A. Dietrich, *"Die Weisen aus dem Morgenlande",* cited in Mary Boyce and Frantz Genet, *A History of Zoroastrianism,* Leiden, Brill, 1991, p. 453, n.449 and *The Archaeological History of Iran,* London, Oxford University Press for the British Academy, 1935, pp.65-66.

Adoration of the Magi: Gestures of Respect

Matthew 2:11

"On coming to the house, they saw the child with his mother Mary, and they bowed down and worshiped him. Then they opened their treasures and presented him with gifts of gold, frankincense and myrrh."

An interesting observation is made by Matthew that the Magi are described as "bowing down." It says they "worshiped him." Some translations indicate "falling down", "kneeling" or "bowing" in the worship of Jesus.

"This gesture, together with the use of kneeling in Luke's birth narrative, had an important effect on Christian religious practices. They were indicative of great respect and typically used when venerating a king. Inspired by these verses, kneeling and prostration were adopted in the early Church. While prostration is now rarely practiced in the West, it is still relatively common in the Eastern Churches, especially during Lent. Kneeling has remained an important element of Christian worship to this day." www.en.wikipedia.org - Biblical Magi.

The Gifts of the Magi:

Was there significance to the gifts of gold, frankincense and myrrh brought by the Magi? The traditional offerings were sheep and calves. According to John Chrysostom, an early Church Father and Archbishop of Constantinople around 400 A.D., the gifts were fit to be given not just to a king but to God. The Magi worshiped Jesus as God.

The Church Father Origin (184-254 A.D.) an early Church father and noted theologian in his *Contra Celsum* says "gold, as to a king; myrrh, as to one who was mortal; and incense, as to a God."

On coming to the house, they saw the child with his mother Mary, and they bowed down and worshiped him.

The Star of Bethlehem: The New Evidence
John C. Iannone

(Three shadowy figures approach the Virgin and child, seated at right. Dating to the mid-third century C.E., this fresco from the Catacomb of Priscilla is the earliest known image of the magi, which later became the most common scene of Jesus' birth and childhood in early Christian art. Photos by Scala/Art Resource.)

What Became of the Magi?

The Scriptures say nothing about the Biblical Magi after reporting that they returned to their own country by a different route, having been warned in a dream about Herod.

There are traditions on where the remains of the Magi are located. Marco Polo in his book *The Book of the*

Million said that he was shown the three tombs of the Magi at Saveh south of Tehran in the 1270's:

> "In Persia is the city of Saba, from which the Three Magi set out and in this city they are buried, in three very large and beautiful monuments, side by side. And above them there is a square building, beautifully kept. The bodies are still entire, with hair and beard remaining." www.en.wikipedia.org - Biblical Magi, p. 12.

Another tradition of a Shrine of the Three Kings places their remains in the Cologne Cathedral. Reputedly, they were first discovered by Saint Helena on her famous pilgrimage to Palestine and the Holy Lands. She took the remains to the Church of the Hagia Sophia in Constantinople. They were moved to Milan and then sent to their current resting place in Cologne.

The Star of Bethlehem: The New Evidence
John C. Iannone

(The Shrine of the Three Kings in the Cathedral of Cologne, Germany)

It is interesting that legends have them buried together since they were from different countries.

Feast of the Epiphany:

The term "Epiphany" means "manifestation" or "revelation." The holiday celebrates the manifestation of Christ to the Gentiles, represented by the Magi. The visit of the Magi is commemorated in Western Churches by the observance of the Epiphany on January 6. The Eastern Orthodox celebrates the visit on December 25th.

How Far Did They Travel?

It is believed the Magi traveled on camels on a trip lasting 4 to 6 months. The Bible is silent on their point of origin. Some scholars assume that they were from Persia and others from Babylon. They might well have travelled close to 1,000 miles or 1,500 km. if from Persia or 550 miles from Babylon. If that assumption is correct we must assume that, even if they themselves didn't walk, most of their bodyguard and retinue would have been on foot. They would have been travelling at the pace of the slowest member of the caravan. If they managed a respectable 20 miles per day, they would have had to travel for 20-50 days to get to Bethlehem. If they made any more extensive stops en route it would, of course, have taken them longer.

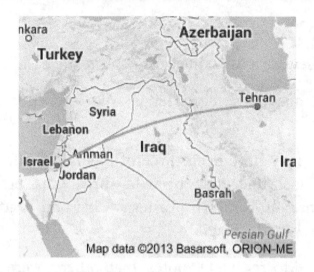

The distance from Tehran in Modern Iran to Jerusalem is approx. 970 miles.

Distance from Bagdad in Iraq (or likely 60 miles south of Bagdad) to Jerusalem 550 miles.

The Star of Bethlehem: The New Evidence
John C. Iannone

SUMMARY:

. . . Matthew says "wise men came from the east."

. . . They may have been kings. We infer this from scriptures.

. . . There may have been three of them. We infer this from the fact that they brought three gifts of gold, frankincense and myrrh. Eastern Christian tradition says there were 12 Magi.

Henry M. Morris, Ph.D. notes that: "there were very likely more than three Magi in the group, probably a dozen or more. They had come from 'the east,' and were themselves representatives of one or more great nations, traveling no doubt with a military escort and a sizable entourage of servants." A sizeable entourage of wise men from the east would likely get the attention of King Herod.

. . . They were "magi" or wise men possibly from the Zoroastrian tradition of the astronomers/astrologers.

. . . They were likely from ancient Iraq (Babylonian land between the Tigris and Euphrates Rivers) although they could have come from ancient Iran or Persia (Parthians).

. . . Their trip was about 550 miles of desert from Babylon or 950 miles of desert if from Persia.

. . . They likely travelled on camels with some in their entourage on foot.

. . . The trip over the deserts lasted several months.

. . . They followed a phenomenon in the heavens learned likely from the Prophet Daniel held captive after the Babylonian captivity.

. . . Matthew 2:2:   The statement of Matthew that *"we saw his star when it rose and have come to worship him"* is perhaps the most intriguing part of Matthew's narrative.

Were the Magi Babylonians or Persians?

Matthew's statement that *"wise men came from the east"* raises the question of whether they were Persians or Babylonians.

On the one hand, we have Anders Hutgard's statement supporting Persia:

> "The Gospel story of the Magi was influenced by an Iranian legend concerning magi and a star, which was connected with Persian beliefs in the rise of a star predicting the birth of a ruler with myths describing the manifestation of a divine figure in fire and light." (Anders Hutgård, *"The Magi and the Star: The Persian Background in Texts and Iconography"*).

On the other hand, it appears more likely that the Magi came from Babylon. There are four points to note in support of this:

1. The Babylonians were clearly familiar with prophesies of a Jewish Messiah from the Prophet Daniel's stay in Babylon during the Babylonian captivity.

2. The Babylonians paid great attention to Jupiter and to Venus as is indicated in the cuneiform *Venus Tablet of Ammisaduqa* dated to the mid-seventeenth century B.C.

3. Babylon and Persia (modern Iraq and Iran) are separated by the formidable Zagros Mountains and the Magi would have had to travel over treacherous terrain if they came from Persia.

4. The Romans and Persians were mortal enemies and the Zagros Mountains separated the two world powers. It seems unlikely that a contingent of Persians would enter Roman territory right into the city of Jerusalem without being challenged.

The Star of Bethlehem: The New Evidence
John C. Iannone

(The Zagros range is 550 miles long and more than 150 miles wide. Situated in what is now Iran, it forms the extreme western boundary of the Iranian plateau. The mountains are a natural barrier, usually snow covered, and traditionally provided the boundary between the early Mesopotamian and Median cultures, the Parthian and Roman empires).

http://www.britannica.com/EBchecked/topic/655360/Zagros-Mountains).

The Star of Bethlehem: The New Evidence
John C. Iannone

CHAPTER NINE

WHAT WAS THE MEANING OF "HIS STAR?"

"Away in a manger,

No crib for His bed

The little Lord Jesus

Laid down His sweet head

The stars in the bright sky

Looked down where He lay

The little Lord Jesus

Asleep on the hay

The cattle are lowing

The poor Baby wakes

But little Lord Jesus

No crying He makes

I love Thee, Lord Jesus

Look down from the sky

And stay by my side,

'Til morning is nigh.

Be near me, Lord Jesus,

I ask Thee to stay

Close by me forever

And love me I pray

Bless all the dear children

In Thy tender care

And take us to heaven

To live with Thee there."

("Away in a Manger" is a Christmas carol first published in the late nineteenth century and used widely throughout the English speaking world. Originally thought to have been written by Martin Luther, it was later shown to have been written, not by him, but in his honor).

The Star of Bethlehem: The New Evidence
John C. Iannone

What was "His Star"?

Matthew 2:2:   *"We saw his star when it rose and have come to worship Him."*

It was a genuine event in the skies which captured the attention of the Magi and it was so meaningful that they set out on a dangerous journey of approximately two to four months over desert terrain and into the territory of the Roman army and of King Herod.

Was this event a comet? A meteor shower? A Supernova? Or a possible conjunction of star and planet.

Was the "Star" a Comet?

There is an inherent problem here in that Comets in ancient times were generally omens of disaster or calamity, hardly in line with the Christmas story.

According to Colin J. Humphreys, Jesus was probably born in 5 B.C., at the time the Chinese recorded a major, new, slow-moving comet -- a "sui-hsing," or star with a sweeping tail in the Capricorn region of the sky. (*"The Star of Bethlehem -- a Comet in 5 BC -- and the Date of the Birth of Christ,"* from *Quarterly Journal of the Royal Astronomical Society* 32, 389-407 (1991).

This is the comet Humphreys believes was called the Star of Bethlehem. However, we now know from the timing of the death of Herod that Jesus was more likely born between 3-2 B.C.

The Tail of Comets:

According to an article in http://csep10.phys.utk.edu on *The General Property of Comets,*

> "The tail of a bright comet can be 150 million kilometers in length, making them the "largest" objects in the Solar System. However, the tail is composed of gas and dust emitted from the nucleus and is very diffuse. The vacuum in the tail is much better than any vacuum we can produce on Earth."

(Courtesy: www.space.com Comets have long tails and are not likely confused with stars).

The article goes on to say:

> "Many comets have two tails, a gas tail (also called the ion tail) composed of ions blown out of the comet away from the Sun by the solar wind, and a dust tail composed of dust particles liberated from the nucleus as the ices are vaporized. The dust particles are left behind in the comet's orbit, and blown slightly away from the Sun by the pressure of the light from the Sun. Thus, they tend to curve relative to the straight

ion tail. The ion tail often shows structure associated with variations in the ejection rate from the nucleus over time. The ion tail is typically bluer in color, narrow, and straight; the dust tail is more diffused, often looks curved, and is more white in color. These differences in appearance are directly correlated with the different sources and compositions of the two tails."

It does not seem is likely that the Magi, students of the heavens, would confuse a comet with a star.

Humphreys says:

"It was not uncommon for magi to visit kings. Magi accompanied King Tiridates of Armenia when he paid homage to Nero, but for magi to have visited Jesus, the astronomical sign must have been powerful. This is why Christmas displays at planetariums show the conjunction of Jupiter and Saturn in 7 B.C."

He continues:

"This is a powerful astronomical sign, but it doesn't satisfy the Gospel description of the Star of Bethlehem as a single star or as one standing over the city, as described by contemporary historians."

He notes that expressions like "'hung over" appear to be uniquely applied in ancient literature to describe a comet. If other evidence emerges showing conjunctions of planets were so described by the ancients, this argument would fail.

Astronomer Dr. John Mosley:

A New York Times article (based on a National Geographic Channel show on the birth) *What Jesus' Birth May Have Looked Like* , cites Dr. John Mosley, from the Griffith Observatory in Los Angeles, who believes "it was a rare conjunction of Venus and Jupiter on June 17, 2 B.C."

Some maintain that it wasn't a "conjunction" because that doesn't satisfy the Gospel description of the Star of Bethlehem as a single star or as one standing over the city, as described by contemporary historians. However, if we understand that what made the star so bright was that there was a conjunction of Jupiter and Regulus making it appear as one star, exceptionally bright, and lasting for a period of time – not to be confused with a comet.

In fact, other evidence does emerge showing just such a conjunction in 3 B.C. of the planet Jupiter (the King Planet) with the star Regulus (The King Star in the Constellation of Leo, the Lion – the symbol of the Tribe of Judah. This would be consistent with the conception of Jesus.

Further, evidence emerges that there was a conjunction nine months later of the very bright planet Venus and Jupiter near Regulus in June 2. B.C. consistent with the birth (Nativity) of Jesus. This **DOUBLE-CONJUNCTION** would, itself, be a marvel of the hand of God.

Humhrey's remarks further that:

> "The two planets had merged into one single gleaming object, one giant star in the sky, in the direction of Jerusalem, as seen from Persia."

Astronomer Sir Patrick Moore noted the only possible explanation for a bright light seen over the Middle East at the time was shooting stars. Sir Patrick, 78, investigated the story of a star guiding three wise men from the East to the village in Judaea for a new book. Stating:

> "Nobody really knows whether there really was a star and it may just be a story - what I have done is look at the scientific evidence for it. This light must have been something which was temporary, spectacular and only seen by a few people - or even King Herod would have known where to look."

"The only thing that fits the bill would be a few shooting stars or a meteor shower across the sky." (www.news.sky.com/story/52858/ *"star-of-bethlehem-a-meteor-shower"*)

He also dismisses the theory of planets moving close together in his book *'The Star Of Bethlehem'*:

"If the three wise men were fooled into thinking a planet like Venus was a star they would not have been very wise."

The Star was not a Meteor Shower:

However, many disagree with Sir Patrick Moore and say that a meteor or meteor shower was not the likely cause because a meteor shower would not look like a star. A meteor would be a fast event, not lingering in the night sky for a long period.

Further, it wasn't a meteor shower because meteors don't rise like stars in the east; neither do they glow long enough nor meet other needed requirements. We say that stars rise in the East because the Earth moves in a counterclockwise direction as see from above the North Pole, making the Sun and Stars appear to rise in the East.

The Star of Bethlehem: The New Evidence
John C. Iannone

The Gospel of Matthew states: "We saw his star when it rose and have come to worship him."

(Time lapse of The Perseid Meteor Shower of 2013)

Was the Star a Supernova?

Andrew Zimmerman Jones, in an article *The Star of Bethlehem - a Physics Overview of the Star of Bethlehem* noted that:

> "In 248 A.D., the Christian writer Origen first proposed the idea that the Bethlehem Star might have been a comet. He suggested the **sui-hsing** (**"broom star"**) noted by Chinese astronomers in 5 B.C., which approximately matches the accurate

date for Jesus' birth (generally calculated at around 4 B.C.)."

Actually, the sui-hsing noted by Chinese astronomers in 5 B.C. was a supernova, not a comet

(May 7, 2007: The brightest stellar explosion ever recorded may be a long-sought new type of supernova, according to observations by NASA's Chandra X-ray Observatory and ground-based optical telescopes. This discovery indicates that violent explosions of extremely massive stars were relatively common in the early universe, and that a similar explosion may be ready to go off in our own galaxy).

"This was a truly monstrous explosion, a hundred times more energetic than a typical supernova," said Nathan Smith of the University of California at Berkeley, who led a team of astronomers from California and the University of Texas in Austin. 'That means the star that exploded might have been as massive as a star can get, about 150 times that of our sun. We've never seen that before.' " www.science.nasa.gov)

Ancient Chinese Astronomy

The Chinese people tended to use astronomy for practical purposes from the very beginning, unlike many of the other cultures studied here that focused mainly on religious aspects of the sky. However, they did develop an extensive system of the zodiac designed to help guide the life of people on Earth. Their version of the zodiac was called the 'yellow path', a reference to the sun traveling along the ecliptic. Like in Western astrology, the Chinese had twelve houses along the yellow path.

The first Chinese written records of astronomy are from about 3000 B.C. The first human record of an eclipse was made in 2136 B.C., and over hundreds of years of advanced sky-watching, the Chinese became very adept at predicting lunar eclipses. They followed a calendar of twelve lunar months, and calculated the year to be 365.25 days long. They translated this 'magic' number into a unit of degrees, by setting the number of degrees in a circle equal to 365.25 (as compared to our use of 360 degrees).   www.starteachastronomy.com /Chinese

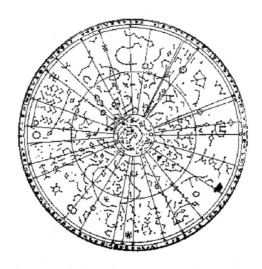

(Ancient Chinese determined seasons and the passage of time through the astronomical phenomena at early evening, mansions -also known as lunar lodges, lunar mansions, constellations, xiu- in the southern sky and the Big Dipper). www.chinapage.com)

The Star was not the Super Nova of 5 B.C.

We have demonstrated in Chapter Five that the thought of the birth of Jesus being somewhere in 5/6 B.C. was based on the incorrect interpretation of a passage in the ancient Jewish historian Josephus which said that King Herod the Great died in 4 B.C., making the birth of Jesus 5/6 B.C. However, the corrected date of Herod's death to early in 1 A.D.

based on a total eclipse of the moon which Josephus was likely referring to in December 29, 1 B.C. makes the birth of Jesus likely in June of 2 B.C. and was in line with the conjunction of the Planets Jupiter and Venus near the King Star Regulus at that time.

Why Didn't Herod's Astronomers/Astrologers see the Star?

I was puzzled over this, but several things came to mind.

Frederick (Rick) Larson, on his website www.bethlehem.star.net makes the observation:

> "The motive of the Magi in coming to Jerusalem tells us a great deal more about them. They wanted to worship a Jewish king. It can't be proven from the text, but it is quite possible that some of the Magi were of Jewish descent, perhaps a Jewish remnant from Daniel's day. This would help explain why a Jewish philosopher, Philo, would admire them, why they were watching the sky for things Jewish, why they wanted to worship a Jewish king, and why they were taken so seriously by Herod and Jewish chief priests. If they were not Jews, then they must have been most impressive magi indeed, as Jews of the time

were deeply disdainful of pagans and their beliefs. They were watching the sky for things Jewish and wanted to worship a Jewish king." This was not something Herod was doing.

In fact, Herod's men MAY have seen the starry phenomenon, but his Court didn't associate it with a Messiah. They weren't looking for this until the Magi pointed it out. Perhaps if they did see the phenomenon, they associated it with Rome's Emperor Caesar Augustus.

The Prophesy of Balaam (Numbers 24: 17-19):

Origen, one of the most influential early Christian theologians, connected the prophecy of Balaam in the Book of Numbers with the Star of Bethlehem.

> "If, then, at the commencement of new dynasties, or on the occasion of other important events, there arises a comet so called, or any similar celestial body, why should it be a matter of wonder that at the birth of Him who was to introduce a new doctrine to the human race, and to make known His teaching not only to Jews, but also to Greeks, and to many of the barbarous nations besides, a star should have arisen? Now I would say, that with respect to comets there is no prophecy in circulation to the effect that such and such a comet was to arise in connection with

a particular kingdom or a particular time; but with respect to the appearance of a star at the birth of Jesus there is a prophecy of Balaam recorded by Moses to this effect: There shall arise a star out of Jacob, and a man shall rise up out of Israel." Adamantius, Origen. "Contra Celsum". Retrieved 2008-06-05., Book I, Chapter LIX.

The prophesy reads as follows:

Number 24: 17-19:

"I see him, but not now;

I behold him, but not near.

A star will come out of Jacob;

a scepter will rise out of Israel.

He will crush the foreheads of Moab,

the skulls of all the people of Sheth.

Edom will be conquered;

Seir, his enemy, will be conquered,

but Israel will grow strong.

A ruler will come out of Jacob

and destroy the survivors of the city."

When They Saw the Star by **Henry M. Morris, Ph.D.**

There is even an ancient tradition that Balaam, the notorious prophet from Mesopotamia, was an early member of the Magi, perhaps even their founder. If so, this fact would at least partially explain why the Magi at the time of Christ were aware that a special star would be used by God to announce the Savior's birth to this world. It was Balaam's prophecy, of course, as recorded in the Bible, that spoke of this future star. Here is his prophecy, actually constrained by God to be uttered against the prophet's own will.

Balaam's reluctant, but divinely inspired, prophecy, revealed that a unique Star associated with Israel would accompany a future Scepter (that is, King) who would eventually rule the world.

Ratzinger notes that Balaam is an historical figure for whom there is extrabibilical confirmation:

> "In 1967, on the East Bank of the Jordan, an inscription was discovered in **which Balaam, son of Beor, is named as a 'seer' of autochthonous deities:** various oracles, both of doom and salvation, are ascribed to him (cf. Hans-Peter Muller, 'Bileam'). The Bible presents him as a soothsayer in the service of the king of Moab, who asks him to curse Israel. Balaam intends to do so, but God himself intervenes, causing the

154

prophet to proclaim a blessing upon Israel instead of a curse. In the biblical tradition he is nevertheless dismissed as an agitator for idolatry and executed (cf: Numbers 31:8; Jos. 13:22)." (Joseph Ratzinger (Pope Benedict XVI), in his book *The Infancy Narratives: Jesus of Nazareth,* p. 91).)

Distinguishing Astronomy and Astrology:

In the ancient world astrology and astronomy were generally treated as one. They were gradually separated in Western 17th century philosophy with the rejection of astrology. During the latter part of the medieval period, astronomy was treated as the foundation upon which astrology could operate.

This happened when astronomers like Copernicus, Johannes Kepler, Galileo and Sir Isaac Newton began to define the science of astronomy and the mathematics and physics of the universe that allowed them to define the three laws of planetary motion, the laws of motion in general (factoring in gravity and inertia) and the clocklike movement of the heavens.

Astrology is often considered in modern times as a pseudo-science which claims that the positions of the heavenly bodies have an effect on the lives of human beings and events on Earth. People studied the motions of the planets and hoped to use them to predict not only the behavior of the heavens, but also wars, natural disasters, the rise and fall of kings, and other earthly matters. However, around the time of Johannes Kepler, Galileo Galilei and Isaac Newton, astronomers came to realize that astrology was basically pseudo-science. From that time on, the primary job of an astronomer was to use mathematics and physics to understand what was going on in the sky.

Astrologers attempt to use the motion of the heavens to predict what was going to happen in our lives. The development of "horoscopes" did precisely that – it was your "sign" that could help predict what was going to happen to a person. There were good omens and bad omens.

****

CHAPTER TEN

RE-CREATING THE HEAVENS IN 3 B.C. - 2 B.C.

"Hark the herald angels sing

Glory to the newborn King!

Peace on earth and mercy mild

God and sinners reconciled

Joyful, all ye nations rise

Join the triumph of the skies

With angelic host proclaim:

Christ is born in Bethlehem

Hark! The herald angels sing

Glory to the newborn King!

Christ by highest heav'n adored

Christ the everlasting Lord!

Late in time behold Him come

Offspring of a Virgin's womb

Veiled in flesh the Godhead see

Hail the incarnate Deity

Pleased as man with man to dwell

Jesus, our Emmanuel

Hark! The herald angels sing

Glory to the newborn King!"

("Hark! The Herald Angels Sing" was written in 1739 by Charles Wesley, the brother of the founder of the Methodist church, John Wesley).

Accomplishments in Astronomy:

To properly lay the foundations of our thesis, we note that the Star of Bethlehem was a real celestial event when the King Star Regulus in the Constellation of Leo, the Lion (the symbol of the Tribe of Judah from which the Messiah would emerge) and the King Planet Jupiter were in alignment during the period of Sept. 3 B.C., the time of Jesus' conception. Further, the King Planet Jupiter and the Mother Planet Venus appeared as one under Regulus in June 2 B.C. at the birth of Jesus. The work of famed astronomers combined with the modern technology of computers enables us to recreate the skies over Jerusalem and Bethlehem in this time period and view these events that startled the Magi. This was a major accomplishment.

Origins of Astronomy:

It is generally thought that the origins of Western astronomy can be found in Mesopotamia, and all Western efforts in the exact sciences are descendants in direct line from the work of the late Babylonian astronomers. This is in line with the story of the Magi, the wise men of the East – likely Babylon or Persia – who were tuned into the heavens and learned from Daniel the Prophet when he was in captivity of the prophesies of the coming Messiah accompanied by signs in the heavens.

(Sumerian Star Chart).

www.crystalinks.com/ SumerianStarChart.jpg

Sumerian Astronomer/Astrologers:

The history of astronomy in Mesopotamia, begins with the Sumerians who developed the earliest known writing system (cuneiform) around 3500–3200 BC. The Sumerian astronomy influenced the Babylonians in Mesopotamia (the delta between the Tigris and Euphrates rivers encompassing modern Iraq). The Sumerian gods played an important role in Mesopotamian mythology and religion.

The Star of Bethlehem: The New Evidence
John C. Iannone

During the 8th and 7th centuries B.C., Babylonian astronomers developed a new empirical approach to astronomy. They began studying philosophy dealing with the ideal nature of the universe and began employing an internal logic within their predictive planetary systems. This was an important contribution to astronomy and the philosophy of science, and some scholars have thus referred to this new approach as the first scientific revolution.

This new approach to astronomy was adopted and further developed in Greek and Hellenistic astronomy. Classical Greek and Latin sources frequently use the term Chaldeans for the astronomers of Mesopotamia, who were, in reality, priest-scribes specializing in astrology and other forms of divination.

Surviving clay fragments of Babylonian astronomy, according to the historian A. Aaboe, show that Babylonian astronomy was:

> "the first and highly successful attempt at giving a refined mathematical description of astronomical phenomena" and that "all subsequent varieties of scientific astronomy, in the Hellenistic world, in India, in Islam, and in the West—if not indeed all subsequent endeavors in the exact sciences—depend upon Babylonian astronomy in decisive and fundamental ways." A.

Aaboe (May 2, 1974). *"Scientific Astronomy in Antiquity".* Philosophical Transactions of the Royal Society 276 (1257): 21–42. (www.en.wikipedia.org - Babylonian Astronomy).

("Other early astronomical documents include astrolabes- clay tablets inscribed with three concentric circles, each one divided up by twelve radii . . . contained the names of constellations. The astrolabes apparently served as star maps, dividing up the visible stars between different sections of the heavens." Mr. Ghaz) - *Mesopotamian Mathematics: Cosmology and Numbers.* February 18, 2011, www.scienceray.com

The Star of Bethlehem: The New Evidence
John C. Iannone

What Happened in the Night Sky over Bethlehem?: Calculating the Mathematics/Physics of the Universe:

The original concept of the ancients was that the universe was "geocentric," that is, that the sun and planets revolved around the earth. Given this concept, modern astronomy could not calculate the position of the stars and planets in the time of Jesus. It would be akin to asking someone to draw a map of the world with Europe in the Pacific. They could never draw an accurate map.

Aristotle (384 BC – 322 BC):

Aristotle believed that the universe was <u>geocentric</u> with the Earth at its center. Classical astronomy followed principles established by Aristotle. He put the earth in the center of the universe and said these elements were below the moon which was the closest celestial body.

> "Aristotle envisioned the earth as the true center of all the circles or 'orbs' carrying the heavenly bodies around it and all motion as 'uniform,' that is, unchanging."
>
> Stanford Encyclopedia of Philosophy <u>www.plato.stanford.edu/entries/copernicus</u>.

Aristotle's Universe

The Greek Philosopher Aristotle

(The diagram of Aristotle's universe above is not to scale, and the planets are aligned for convenience in illustration; generally they were distributed around the spheres.) The sphere of the stars lay beyond the ones shown here for the planets. In the Aristotelian conception there was an outermost sphere that was the domain of the "Prime Mover." The Prime Mover caused the outermost sphere to rotate at constant angular velocity, and this motion was imparted from sphere to sphere, thus causing the whole thing to rotate).

www.csep10.phys.utk.edu.
astr161/lect/retrograde/aristotle.html

Ptolemy (c. AD 90 – c. AD 168):

In the second century, the Roman astronomer Ptolemy compiled his *Almagest* and also postulated the Earth as the center of our solar system

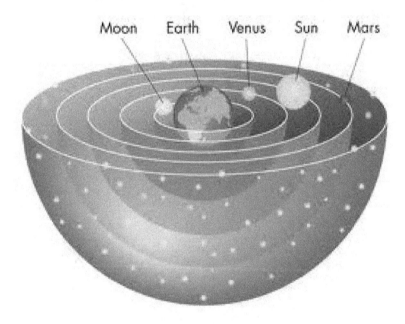

www.3quarksdaily.com

Nicolaus Copernicus (1473 – 1543):

Copernicus is credited with discovering that the Universe is <u>heliocentric,</u> with the sun at its center. His theory, however, sees these orbits as **circles,** a problem which would be clarified with Johannes Kepler who postulated that planets move in **ellipses**. Let's first discuss Nicolaus Copernicus.

Copernicus was a Polish mathematician and astronomer who proposed that the sun was stationary in the center of the universe and the earth revolved around the sun (the Heliocentric thesis). He was disturbed by the failure of Ptolemy's geocentric model. In the Stanford Encyclopedia of Philosophy (www.plato.stanford.edu/enteire/copernicus), the authors note that:

> "at the time, Copernicus's heliocentric idea was very controversial, but it was the start of a change in the way the world was viewed and Copernicus came to be seen as the initiator of the Scientific Revolution."

Sometime between 1510 and 1514 he wrote an essay that came to be known as the *Commentariolus* (MW 75-126) and his book *On The Revolutions of the Heavenly Bodies,* in which he introduced his new cosmological idea of a heliocentric solar system with the planets moving around the sun.

The Star of Bethlehem: The New Evidence
John C. Iannone

In an article *"The Copernican Model: A Sun-Centered Solar System"* we find an excellent summary of Copernicus' discovery:

> "In this new ordering the Earth is just another planet (the third outward from the Sun), and the Moon is in orbit around the Earth, not the Sun. The stars are distant objects that do not revolve around the Sun. Instead, the Earth is assumed to rotate once in 24 hours, causing the stars to appear to revolve around the Earth in the opposite direction."

("To know that we know what we know, and to know that we do not know what we do not know, that is true knowledge. ~ Nicolaus Copernicus)

Note: Copernicus made his discovery without the aid of a telescope!

www.csep10.phy.utk/edu/astr161/lect/retrograde/comer
nican.html

In this same article, the author notes:

> "Three incorrect ideas held back the development of modern astronomy from the time of Aristotle until the 16th and 17th centuries:
>
> (1)   The assumption that the Earth was the center of the Universe;
>
> (2)   The assumption of uniform circular motion in the heavens;
>
> (3)   The assumption that objects in the heavens were made from a perfect, unchanging substance not found on Earth."

Copernicus challenged assumption Number 1 but not assumption Number 2. He believed the sun was the center of the universe but that the planets moved in circles around the sun. Astronomy had not yet mastered the mathematics and physics of the universe.

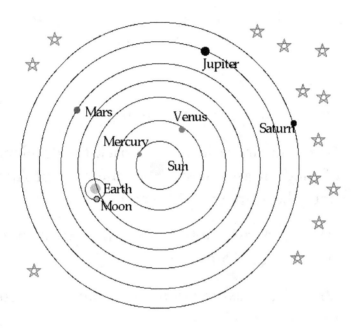

www.google.com/#q=copernicus+model+of+the+univ
erse

The Star of Bethlehem: The New Evidence
John C. Iannone

The Copernican Revolution in Science:

The Copernican Revolution was one of the greatest in Western civilization. Although his ideas remained rather obscure for about 100 years after his death,, the work of Kepler, Galileo and Newton would "sweep away completely the ideas of Aristotle (and Ptolemy) and replace them with the modern view of astronomy and natural science."

Interestingly, part of Copernicus' thinking was that equally spaced planets in circular orbits would represent harmony in the universe. Copernicus had made no observations and stated no general laws.

Of course, we came to learn through others like Johannes Kepler that the planets were neither equally spaced or in circular orbits, but Copernicus' theory was a major step forward in astronomy.

Tycho Brahe (1546-1601) was the greatest astronomical observer before the invention of the telescope. He called Copernicus a 'second Ptolemy'." However, Copernicus' theory was quite controversial in this period. As an example, Martin Luther made disparaging comments about Copernicus because the idea of a heliocentric universe seemed to contradict the Bible.

Further, some writers among them John Donne and William Shakespeare: "were the most influential who

171

feared that Copernicus' theory . . . destroyed hierarchal natural order which would in turn destroy social order and bring about chaos." (Eric Weisstein: on Copernicus. www.scienceworld.wolfram.com/biography/Copernicus. html.

It was certainly changing times!

Aristarchus of Samos (310 BC – ca. 230 BC)

It should be pointed out that a sun-centered Solar System had been proposed as early as about 200 B.C. by Aristarchus of Samos (Samos is an island off the coast of what is now Turkey). However, his theory did not survive long under the weight of Aristotle's influence. Unfortunately, we would have to wait almost 1,700 years until Copernicus was able to present his theory in a more dramatic and acceptable way.

Johannes Kepler – The Elliptical Path of Planets (1571 – 1630):

The next great stride forward in defining the mathematics and physics of the universe that would allow us to eventually use computers to map the heavens at the time of Jesus was taken by Johannes Kepler.

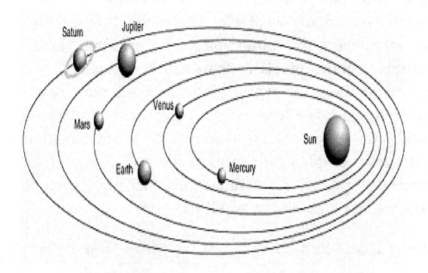

Courtesy: www.universetoday.com

Kepler demonstrates that the movement of the planets around the sun (heliocentric concept) was <u>not circular, but elliptical</u>, paving the way for his theory defining the Three Laws of Planetary Motion.

Kepler firmly believed in the Copernican system. However, Kepler was able to provide a major piece of the puzzle. He came to the realization that the orbits of the planets were not the circles of Aristotle and assumed implicitly by Copernicus, but were <u>instead the "flattened circles" that we call ellipses, and, further, that the Sun was not in the center of the ellipse.</u>

Kepler was able to utilize the work of his predecessor Tyco Brahe, a Danish nobleman, (1546-1601), who made important contributions by devising the most precise instruments available before the invention of the telescope for observing the heavens. Brahe determined more precisely than had been possible the detailed motions of the planets. In particular, Brahe compiled extensive data on the planet Mars, which would later prove crucial to Kepler in his formulation of the laws of planetary motion because it would be sufficiently precise to demonstrate that the orbit of Mars was not a circle but an ellipse.

www.csep10.phys.utk.edu/astr161/lect/history/kepler.html.

Kepler's Three Laws of Planetary Motion:

Kepler eventually built his Three Laws of Planetary Motion utilizing the voluminous and precise data of Brahe.

Here are his Three Laws of Planetary Motion that serve, along with Sir Isaac Newton's work, as the basis for modern calculations of the ancient skies:

1. The orbits of the planets are ellipses with the sun at one focus of the ellipse.

2. The line joining the planet to the Sun sweeps out equal areas in equal times as the planet travels around the ellipse.
3. The ratio of the squares of the revolutionary periods for two planets is equal to the ratio of the cubes of their semi-major axes.

While I do not profess to understand the mathematics here, scientists agree it represented a major breakthrough in defining the mathematics and physics of the solar system and pointed out the precision with which the universe works like a great clock. We as Christians believe this is the work of God's hand.

Galileo Galilei (1564-1642):

It was left to Galileo and Sir Isaac Newton to advance the work of Kepler and lay the foundations of our ability to recreate the ancient skies with the advent of computers and the data provided by these astronomers and physicists.

> "Galileo . . . provided the crucial observations that proved the Copernican hypothesis and also laid the foundations for a correct understanding of how objects moved on the surface of the earth (dynamics) and of gravity."

"Newton, who was born the same year Galileo died, would build on Galileo's ideas to demonstrate that <u>the laws of motion in the heavens and the laws of motion on the earth were one and the same.</u> Thus, Galileo began and Newton completed a synthesis of astronomy and physics in which the former was recognized as but a particular example of the latter and that would banish the notions of Aristotle almost completely from both."

www.csep10.phys.utk.edu/astr161/lect/history/galileo.html

The Telescope:

It is interesting that Copernicus and Kepler did not have the advantage of the telescope but were able to do the calculations that revolutionized astronomy and physics and paved the way for our current understanding of the heavens at the time of Jesus.

The Star of Bethlehem: The New Evidence
John C. Iannone

(www.abcnews.go.com)

Dutch spectacle makers receive the credit for the invention of the telescope and Galileo was the first to use the telescope to study the heavens systematically.

> "His little telescope was poorer than even a cheap modern amateur telescope, but what he observed in the heavens rocked the very foundations of Aristotle's universe and the theological-philosophical worldview that it supports. It is said that what Galileo saw was so disturbing for some officials of the Church that they refused to even look through his telescope; they reasoned that the Devil was capable of making anything appear in the telescope, so it was best not to look through it."

www.csep10.phys.utk.edu/astr161/lect/history/galileo.html

Sir Isaac Newton (1642 - 1727)

The addition of the understanding of gravity was of vital importance in the work of Sir Isaac Newton and the completion of the model. When Galileo understood the principle behind the fact that two objects of very different weight would hit the ground at the same time when dropped, he helped Newton to formulate a theory of gravitation.

Newton is credited with "The Great Synthesis" combining:

1. The Three Laws of Motion;
2. The Theory of Universal Gravitation, and
3. The demonstration that Kepler's Laws follow from the Law of Gravitation.

Kepler's laws apply only to the motions of the planets but say nothing about any other motion in the Universe.

The Star of Bethlehem: The New Evidence
John C. Iannone

(Sir Isaac Newton. Note the apple on the tree. Newton supposedly determined his laws of gravitation by studying an apple falling from a tree. www.sirisaacnewton.info)

However, Newton added an important element:

> "First, he demonstrated that the motion of objects on the Earth could be described by three new Laws of Motion, and then he went on to show that Kepler's three Laws of Planetary Motion were special cases of Newton's three Laws if a force of a particular kind (that we now call gravitational force) were postulated to exist between all objects in the universe having mass."

http://cesp10.phys.utk.edu

Newton's Third law stated:

> "To every action there is always an equal and opposite reaction (or) the forces of two bodies are equal, opposite and collinear."

> Newton's Law of Universal Gravitation stated:

> "Every point mass in the universe attracts every other point mass with a force that is directly proportional to the product of their masses and inversely proportional to the square of the distance between them."

This is a lot to grasp, but was the final piece of the puzzle started by Copernicus and advanced by Brahe, Kepler and Galileo.

Why is all this important to our thesis?

The work of these men (Copernicus, Kepler, Galileo and Newton) developed a precise mathematical and physical model of the universe and it's precise clocklike movements over the centuries. The rise of the modern computer gave us the ability to crunch vast amounts of data into our computers and actually reverse the motions of the heavens with these formulas and thereby recreate the skies in past centuries, including the skies over Bethlehem and Jerusalem in the period of Jesus' birth.

Charting the Birth of Jesus:

Given all the data discussed, we can chart out the sequence of historical data correlating with the science of astronomy as follows:

. . . Caesar Augustus is Emperor – Pax Romana at Jesus' birth.

. . . A Census is ordered under Quitilius – Legate of Syria (3-2 B.C.)

. . . September 3 B.C. Jesus is conceived (Incarnation)

There is a conjunction of the King Planet Jupiter with the King Star Regulus in the Constellation of the Leo the Lion – the symbol of the Tribe of Judah from which the Messiah would come.

. . . Sometime before June 2 B.C. Joseph & Mary go to Bethlehem to comply with demands of the Roman Census.

. . . June 2 B.C. (a likely date is the 17^t) Jesus is born in Bethlehem (Nativity).

. . . This is consistent with the Shepherd living in the fields during the "lambing season" in the Spring/Summer.

The Star of Bethlehem: The New Evidence
John C. Iannone

. . . At this time, there is a conjunction of the King Planet Jupiter with the Planet Venus (symbolic of the Mother of Jesus) that appeared so brightly in the night sky that it caught the attention of the Magi to pursue the phenomenon of what appeared to be one bright star.

. . . Likely between June, 2 B.C. – Dec. 29, 1 B.C. the Magi come to Bethlehem to visit the "house" of Jesus who is a "toddler" (Paidon in Greek) following a Star from the East.

. . . Believing this child to be under two years, Herod orders the killing of the children under 2 years old to eliminate any potential rival to the throne

. . . Shortly thereafter on Dec. 29, 1 B.C. there is a total eclipse of the Moon which is the eclipse that Josephus likely refers to in *Antiquities* just before Herod's death.

. . . King Herod the Great dies about two months later in 1 A.D.

There is a precise historical and astronomical correlation between the Conception of Jesus, the Census, the Birth of Jesus, the Magi, the Slaughter of the Innocents and the Death of Herod just after the total lunar eclipse of Dec. 29, 1 B.C.

The Star of Bethlehem: The New Evidence
John C. Iannone

John Pratt *"Yet Another Eclipse for Herod"* The Planetarian, identifies the date at June 17, 2 B.C. and far exceeds the others as being truly outstanding because of the conjunction of Jupiter and Venus:

> "The conjunction of Jupiter and Venus on June 17, 2 B.C. was so close that the two planets would have appeared to touch each other. Calculations indicate that there has never been a brighter, close conjunction of Venus and Jupiter so near to the bright star Regulus in the Constellation of Leo in the 2000 years before or since."

> He is supported in this by Astronomer Dr. John Mosley from the Griffith Observatory in Los Angeles. (See: New York Times article (based on a National Geographic Channel show on the birth) *What Jesus' Birth May Have Looked Like* .

****

The Star of Bethlehem: The New Evidence
John C. Iannone

CHAPTER ELEVEN

SUMMARIZING THE EVIDENCE

"O Holy Night! The stars are brightly shining,

It is the night of our dear Savior's birth.

Long lay the world in sin and error pining.

Till He appeared and the Soul felt its worth.

A thrill of hope the weary world rejoices,

For yonder breaks a new and glorious morn.

Fall on your knees! Oh, hear the angel voices!

O night divine, O night when Christ was born;

O night, O Holy Night , O night divine!

O night, O Holy Night , O night divine!

Led by the light of faith serenely beaming,

With glowing hearts by His cradle we stand.

O'er the world a star is sweetly gleaming,

185

Now come the wise men from out of the Orient land.

The King of kings lay thus lowly manger;

In all our trials born to be our friends.

He knows our need, our weakness is no stranger,

Behold your King! Before him lowly bend!

Behold your King! Before him lowly bend!"

(The words and lyrics of the old carol 'O Holy Night' were written by Placide Cappeau de Roquemaure in 1847. Cappeau was a wine seller by trade but was asked by the parish priest to write a poem for Christmas. He obliged and wrote the beautiful words of the hymn. He then realized that it should have music to accompany the words and he approached his friend Adolphe Charles Adams (1803-1856).

Summarizing the Evidence

Over the years there have been many misconceptions about what really happened in the skies over Babylon and Jerusalem/Bethlehem during this period of Jesus' birth - misconceptions that distorted the truth of the

The Star of Bethlehem: The New Evidence
John C. Iannone

Gospels. To some, the Star is a myth. Many thought Herod died in 4 B.C. Others said there was no Census at that time, etc., etc. all attempting to mythologize the events surrounding the great handiwork of God in giving tribute to the birth of His son.

However, let's look at the facts that have now come to light to determine what set of events most fits what we believe to be the truth behind the events surrounding the birth of Jesus and the real presence of heavenly phenomenon we call the Star of Bethlehem.

What do we now know?

. . .Caesar Augustus was the Emperor ushering in a period of unprecedented peace: the Pax Romana.

. . .There was, in fact, a Census taken under Publius Quintilius, the Legate of Syria supporting the Gospel of Luke:

John P. Pratt's article *"Yet Another Eclipse for Herod,"* The Planetarium, Vol. 19, No. 4, Dec. 1990, pp. 8-14, points out that there was, in fact, an Empire-Wide Registration. There was:

> " . . . a combined census and oath of allegiance to Augustus Caesar in 3 B.C. -2 B.C. perhaps related to the bestowal of the title **'pater patriae'** (**Father of Thy Country**) by the Roman Senate on

February 5, 2 B.C." (Res Gestae 35; Ovid, Fasti 2, 129).

He cites Orosius (a fifth century historian) clearly linking an oath to the registration at the birth of Christ:

> "Augustus ordered that a census be taken of each province everywhere and that all men be enrolled. So at that time, Christ was born and was entered on the Roman census list as soon as he was born. This is the earliest and most famous public acknowledgment which market Caesar as the first of all men and the Romans as lords of the world . . . that first and greatest census was taken, since in this one name of Caesar all the peoples of the great nations took oath, and at the same time, through **the participation in the census, were made part of one society.**"

(Orosius, Adv. Pag. V1 22.7, V11.2.16 by Deferrari, R.J. The Fathers of the Church (Washington, D.C.: Catholic U. Press, 1964, Vol. 50, p. 281, 287).

The Lunar eclipse mentioned by Josephus was most likely the Lunar eclipse of December 29, 1 B.C.

The Star of Bethlehem: The New Evidence
John C. Iannone

It is worth repeating the quote from *"Solar and Lunar Eclipses of the Ancient Near East"*, by M. Kudlek and E. Mickler (1971) they mention:

"Lunar Eclipses Visible in Palestine:

. . . 7 B.C. No eclipses

. . . 6 B.C. No eclipses

. . . 5 B.C. March 23. Total eclipse. Central at 8:30 pm (elapsed time between eclipse and Passover: twenty-nine days).

. . . 5 B.C. September 15. Total eclipse. Central at 10:30 pm (elapsed time between eclipse and Passover: seven months).

. . . 4 B.C. March 13. Partial eclipse. Central at 2:20 am (elapsed time between eclipse and Passover: twenty-nine days (Note: this is the eclipse referred to by Whiston. However, it does not fit the history because the short period of 29 days between the eclipse and Passover does not allow sufficient time for the many events recorded between the partial eclipse and Passover.

. . . 3 B.C. No eclipses

. . . 2 B.C. No eclipses

. . . 1 B.C. January 10. Total eclipse. Central at 1:00 am (elapsed time between eclipse and Passover: twelve and a half weeks).

. . . 1 B.C. December 29. A second total eclipse and likely the one referred to by Josephus."

Since Josephus mentioned a number of events that transpired between the eclipse assumed by some authors to be 4 B.C. and the Passover 29 days later, many authors have noted that it was virtually impossible for all these events to take place during this period after the partial eclipse, and therefore that Josephus was NOT talking about the eclipse of 4 B.C. but that he was talking of the Total Eclipse on December 29, 1 B.C. This would mean that Herod, who died about two months after this eclipse, died in/about February 1 A.D.

Support of a later date for the death of Herod is outlined by other scholars. Since the work of Emil Schürer in 1896, most scholars had agreed that Herod died at the end of March or early April in 4 B.C. However, Schürer's consensus has not gone unchallenged in the 20th century, with several scholars endorsing 1 A.D. as the year of Herod's death:

The Star of Bethlehem: The New Evidence
John C. Iannone

Scholars challenging 4 B.C. include:

. . . Edwards, Ormond. *"Herodian Chronology"*, Palestine Exploration Quarterly 114 (1982) 29–42

. . . Filmer, W. E. *"Chronology of the Reign of Herod the Great"*, Journal of Theological Studies ns 17 (1966), 283–298.

. . . Keresztes, Paul. *Imperial Rome and the Christians: From Herod the Great to About 200 AD* (Lanham, Maryland: University Press of America, 1989), pp.1–43.

. . . Vardaman, Jerry; Yamauchi, Edwin M., eds. (1989). *"The Nativity and Herod's Death"*. Chronos, Kairos, Christos: *Nativity and Chronological Studies* Presented to Jack Finegan (Winona Lake, Indiana: Eisenbrauns): 85–92.

. . . Finegan, Jack. *Handbook of Biblical Chronology*, Rev. ed. (Peabody, MA: Hendrickson, 1998) 300, §516.

We note that:

. . .Herod ordered the slaughter of the innocents, children 2 and under, before his death.

This would indicate that Jesus was about 1-2 years old, more likely 1 ½ years old. Matthew indicated that the Magi saw the "child" and uses the term paidon (παιδίον) which in biblical Greek meant a young child, a toddler.

The Star of Bethlehem: The New Evidence
John C. Iannone

. . . This would put the birth of Jesus around June of 2 B.C. and the pregnancy or conception of Jesus (called in Catholic Theology the Incarnation) nine months earlier in September 3 B.C.

. . . The findings of the 6th century Monk Dionysius Exiguus were very close to the correct date which he said was Dec. 25, 1 B.C.

. . . The astronomical facts demonstrate that on June 17, 2 B.C. there was very bright conjunction of the King Star Planet Jupiter with the Planet Venus – symbolic of Mary, the Mother.

We believe this conjunction, and not the conjunction mentioned by Joseph Ratzinger (Pope Benedict XVI) in his work *The Infancy Narratives: Jesus of Nazareth*, is more likely the conjunction referred to. Pope Benedict quoted Konradin Ferrari d'Occhieppo who stated that:

> "the conjunction of the planets Jupiter and Saturn in the constellation of Pisces in the years 7-6 B.C. – now believed to be the actual time of Jesus' birth – is something that the Babylonian astronomers could have calculated."

I believe that (placing the conjunctions side by side) the conjunction of Jupiter and Saturn in the Constellation of Pisces has little theological significance from an astronomical point of view versus the conjunction of the King Planet Jupiter and the Mother Planet Venus near the King Star Regulus in the Constellation of Leo, the Lion – the symbol of the Tribe of Judah from whom the Messiah would come.

The conjunction of Jupiter and the King Star Regulus in September B.C. most fits the period of the conception of Jesus).

The conjunction of Jupiter and Venus in June 2 B.C. nine months later best supports the time of the birth of Jesus (Nativity).

The Star of Bethlehem: The New Evidence
John C. Iannone

The Mother Planet 'Venus' and the King Planet 'Jupiter' came into conjunction three times from the summer of 3 BC through the fall of 2 BC including the closest conjunction ever recorded.

http://isaiah612.blogspot.com/2009_08_01_archive.html

Scientific and Historic Validation of Scripture:

It would appear then that the birth of Jesus was likely on or extremely close to June 17, 2 B.C. when the King Star Jupiter and the Planet Venus were in <u>the closest conjunction of these planets ever recorded</u>. His conception was on/about September 17, 3 B.C. with the conjunction of the King Planet Jupiter and the King Star Regulus in the Constellation of Leo, the Lion.

The Star of Bethlehem: The New Evidence
John C. Iannone

These events in the night skies attracted the Magi to look to the heavens and constituted what became known as the Star of Bethlehem. The conjunction of the heavens at that time, an unfathomable mystery clearly pointing to the hand of God, gives historical and scientific validation to our faith throughout the centuries that Jesus is, in fact, the Son of God, born under the Star/Planets conjunction ordered by His Father.

The Coronation:

Rick Larson makes an interesting observation of a "coronation." It appeared that in the period between 3 B.C. - 2 B.C. Jupiter entered into retrograde at least three times, appearing to "crown" Regulus.

> "In 3/2 B.C., Jupiter's retrograde wandering would have called for our magus' full attention. After Jupiter and Regulus had their king encounter, Jupiter continued on its path through the star field. But then it entered retrograde. It 'changed its mind' and headed back to Regulus for a second conjunction. After this second pass it reversed course again for yet a third rendezvous with Regulus, a triple conjunction. A triple pass like this is more rare. Over a period of months, our watching magus would have seen the Planet

of Kings dance out a halo above the Star of Kings. A coronation."

(Rick Larson, *The Starry Dance.* www.bethlehemstar.net/dance.

What is Retrograde?

Retrograde is defined as: "the apparent backward motion of a planet viewed from Earth. To clarify, the normal direction of Planets from our perspective is west to east. Retrograde motion is when a planet starts moving (or appears to move) in the opposite direction." www.learningastronomy.com

We see this in daily life if we are driving a car (let's say at 60 mph) and we pass someone on a bicycle moving in the same direction at 10 mph. As we pass the bicyclist it appears that he/she is moving backward when in reality the individual is moving forward in the same direction but at a slower speed.

An Unfathomable Double-Conjunction:

What is most fascinating about the sequence of events from 3 B.C. to 2 B.C. is the fact that there was a **double conjunction** pointing to the conception (Incarnation) of Jesus and His birth (Nativity) occurring nine months apart.

The odds of one conjunction is rare. The odds of a double-conjunction signifying both the conception and birth of Jesus is super extraordinary. Other than the direct hand of God in the movement of the Heavens, there doesn't seem to be any other explanation.

Example of Retrograde of Planet Mars:

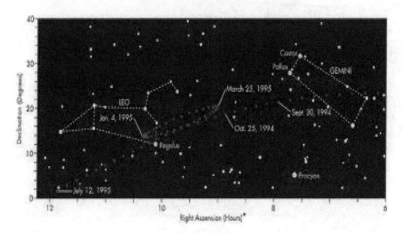

("One particularly baffling aspect of planetary wanderings is the periods of retrograde motion. A planet such as Mars would spend much of the year moving slowly eastward against the background of fixed stars. Then . . . it would change direction and slide westward for a couple of months or so before stopping again and returning to its easterly path. This is retrograde motion (retro meaning backward). The image above traces the positions of the planet Mars as it executed a retrograde loop in 1995." www.mhhe.com)

The Star of Bethlehem: The New Evidence
John C. Iannone

The Star of Bethlehem: The New Evidence
John C. Iannone

CHARTING THE SEQUENCE OF EVENTS

(John C. Iannone)

< --------18 Months--------→

Sept. 3 BC	June 2 BC	Dec. 29, 1 BC	Herod dies 1 AD
.KingPlanet Jupiter	. King Planet Jupiter .	Total Eclipse	Herod dies
& King Star Regulus	& Mother Planet Venus		
In Conjunction	in Conjunction		
In Leo the Lion,	in Leo the Lion,		

(Symbol of Tribe of Judah from which Messiah would come).

CONCEPTION	BIRTH	VISIT OF
OF JESUS	OF JESUS	MAGI

Caesar Augustus - Emperor

Census of 3 - 2 B.C.   a. Magi set out to follow "star."

b. Magi visit house of Mary/Joseph

and worship child Toddler.

c. Mary & Joseph flee to Egypt

d. Magi warned about Herod in dream

e. Herod kills the "innocents"

f. Herod dies

****

The Star of Bethlehem: The New Evidence
John C. Iannone

AFTER FORWARD

WHY DO WE CELEBRATE CHRISTMAS ON

DECEMBER 25TH?

The work of astronomy demonstrates that the Star of Bethlehem represented real phenomena in the skies in 3 B.C. - 2 B.C and that Jesus was, in fact, born in June of 2 B.C.

Why, then, do we celebrate on December 25th?

The Bible offers few clues: Celebrations of Jesus' Nativity are not mentioned in the Gospels or Acts; the date is not given although the time of year is alluded to in Luke's statement that the "shepherds were living in the fields." The biblical reference to shepherds tending their flocks and living in the fields when they hear the news of Jesus' birth (Luke 2:8) suggests the Spring lambing season.

Andrew McGowan, President of Trinity College at the University of Melbourne, Australia, notes:

The Star of Bethlehem: The New Evidence
John C. Iannone

"The extra biblical evidence from the first and second century is equally sparse: There is no mention of birth celebrations in the writings of early Christian writers such as Irenaeus (c. 130–200) or Tertullian (c. 160–225). Origen of Alexandria (c. 165–264) goes so far as to mock Roman celebrations of birth anniversaries, dismissing them as "pagan" practices—a strong indication that Jesus' birth was not marked with similar festivities at that place and time. As far as we can tell, Christmas was not celebrated at all at this point."

"How December 25 Became Christmas" www.biblicalarchaeology.org

McGowan continues:

"By the fourth century, however, we find references to two dates that were widely recognized—and now also celebrated—as Jesus' birthday: December 25 in the western Roman Empire and January 6 in the East (especially in Egypt and Asia Minor). The modern Armenian Church continues to celebrate Christmas on January 6; for most Christians, however, December 25 would prevail, while January 6 eventually came to be known as the Feast of the Epiphany, commemorating the arrival of the magi in Bethlehem. The period between became the holiday season later known as the 12 days of Christmas . . . . So, almost 300 years after Jesus was born, we finally find people observing his birth in mid-winter. But how had they settled on the dates December 25 and January 6th? "

December 25th borrowed from pagan celebrations?

McGovern notes that the most widely held view of why Dec. 25th was chosen is that it was borrowed from pagan celebrations. The Romans had their mid-winter Saturnalia festival in late December; barbarian peoples of northern and western Europe kept holidays at similar times. In 274 A.D, the Roman emperor Aurelian established a feast of the birth of Sol Invictus (the Unconquered Sun), on December 25. Christmas, the argument goes, is really a spin-off from these pagan solar festivals. According to this theory, early Christians deliberately chose these dates to encourage the spread of Christmas and Christianity throughout the Roman world: If Christmas looked like a pagan holiday, more pagans would be open to both the holiday and the God whose birth it celebrated.

A marginal note on a manuscript of the writings of the Syriac biblical commentator Dionysius bar-Salibi states that;

"in ancient times the Christmas holiday was actually shifted from January 6 to December 25 so that it fell on the same date as the pagan Sol Invictus holiday. In the 18th and 19th centuries, Bible scholars spurred on by the new study of comparative religions latched on to this idea. They claimed that because the early Christians didn't know when Jesus was born, they simply assimilated the pagan solstice festival for their own purposes, claiming it as the time of the Messiah's birth and celebrating it accordingly."

"More recent studies have shown that many of the holiday's modern trappings do reflect pagan customs borrowed much later, as Christianity expanded into northern and Western Europe. The Christmas tree, for example, has been linked with late medieval druidic practices. This has only encouraged modern audiences to assume that the date, too, must be pagan."

"After Constantine converted to Christianity we do find Christians deliberately adapting and Christianizing pagan festivals. A famous proponent of this practice was Pope Gregory the Great, who, in a letter written in 601 A.D. to a Christian missionary in Britain, recommended that local pagan temples not be destroyed but be converted into churches, and that pagan festivals be celebrated as feasts of Christian martyrs. At this late point, Christmas may well have acquired some pagan trappings. But we don't have evidence of Christians adopting pagan festivals in the third century, at which point dates for Christmas were established. Thus, it seems unlikely that the date was simply selected to correspond with pagan solar festivals."

In her article *Why Do Christians Celebrate Christmas on December 25?*, Mary Fairchild talks about the word *Christmas or The Mass of Christ*:

Fairchild notes that:

"The term Christmas appeared in Old English as early as 1038 A.D. as Cristes Maesse, and later as Cristes-messe in A.D. 1131. It means "the Mass of Christ." This name was established by the Christian church to disconnect the holiday and its customs from its pagan origins. As one fourth century theologian penned, "We hold this day holy, not like the pagans because of the birth of the sun, but because of He who made it."

"Although it is true that many traditional Christmas customs find their origins in pagan practices, these ancient and forgotten associations are far removed from the hearts of Christian worshipers today at Christmas time. So much so, it seems a pointless concern. If the focus of Christmas is Jesus Christ and his gift of eternal life, then what harm can come from such a celebration? Moreover, Christian churches see Christmas as an occasion to spread the good news of the gospel at a time when many unbelievers pause to consider Christ."

(http://christianity.about.com/od/christmas)

Origins of The Christmas Tree:

As noted by McGowan above:

"The Christmas tree . . . has been linked with late medieval druidic practices. This has only encouraged modern audiences to assume that the date, too, must be pagan."

A different view is expressed by the writers of Encyclopædia Britannica;

"While it is clear that the modern Christmas tree originates in Renaissance and early modern Germany, there are a number of speculative theories as to its ultimate origin. Its 16th-century origins are sometimes associated with Protestant Christian reformer Martin Luther who, according to the TV channel History, 'first added lighted candles to a tree.' "

"According to the Encyclopædia Britannica, "The use of evergreen trees, wreaths, and garlands to symbolize eternal life was a custom of the ancient Egyptians, Chinese, and Hebrews. Tree worship was common among the pagan Europeans and survived their conversion to Christianity in the Scandinavian customs of decorating the house and barn with evergreens at the New Year to scare away the devil and of setting up a tree for the birds during Christmastime."

http://en.wikipedia.org/wiki/Christmas_tree

****

The Star of Bethlehem: The New Evidence
John C. Iannone

The Author welcomes comments at:

jciannone@gmail.com

BIBLIOGRAPHY

Aaboe, A., *"Scientific Astronomy in Antiquity"*. Philosophical Transactions of the Royal Society (May 2, 1974).

Bishop Eusebius, *Church History*, Book V.

Boyce, Boyce and Frantz Genet, *A History of Zoroastrianism*, Leiden, Brill, 1991, and *The Archaeological History of Iran.*

London, Oxford University Press for the British Academy, 1935, pp.65-66.

Collins English Dictionary – Complete and Unabridged © HarperCollins Publishers 1991, 1994, 1998, 2000, and 2003.

Copernicus, Nicolaus, *Commentariolus (MW 75-126)* and *On The Revolutions of the Heavenly Bodies.*

Dietrich, A., *Die Weisen aus dem Morgenlande.*

Mosley, Dr. John (See New York Times article below)

Fairchild, Mary, *Why Do Christians Celebrate Christmas on December 25th?*

Fairchild, Mary, *The Star of Bethlehem* (www.About.com - Christianity.

Ferrari d'Occhieppo, Konradin, *Der Stern von Bethlehem.*

Filmer, W. E. *"Chronology of the Reign of Herod the Great"*, Journal of Theological Studies ns 17 (1966), 283–298.

Finegan, Jack. Handbook of Biblical Chronology, Rev. ed. (Peabody, MA: Hendrickson, 1998) 300, §516.

Ghaz, Mr. - *Mesopotamian Mathematics: Cosmology and Numbers.*

Gospel of St. Luke *Chapter 2*

Gospel of St. Matthew *Chapter 2*

Hutgård, Anders, *"The Magi and the Star: The Persian Background in Texts and Iconography".*

Hughes, David, *The Star of Bethlehem.*

Josephus: *The Jewish Wars.*

Josephus: *Antiquities of the Jews.*

Keresztes, Paul, *Imperial Rome and the Christians: From Herod the Great to About 200 AD,* (Lanham, Maryland: University Press of America, 1989), pp.1–43.

Kudlek, M. and E. Mickler, *"Solar and Lunar Eclipses of the Ancient Near East",* (1971).

Larson, Rick: DVD: The Star of Bethlehem produced by Stephen McEveety (The Passion of the Christ).

Larson, Rick, "The Starry Dance, " www.bethlehemstar.net.

Larson, Rick – The Star of Bethlehem DVD

Morris, Henry M., Ph.D., *When They Saw the Star.*

New American Standard Hebrew-Aramaic and Greek dictionary.

New York Times article (based on a National Geographic Channel show on the birth) *What Jesus' Birth May Have Looked Like* , citing Dr. John Mosley from the Griffith Observatory.

Novak, Ralph, *Christianity and the Roman Empire: Background Texts.*

Origen, Adamantius, "*Contra Celsum*". *Retrieved 2008-06-05., Book I, Chapter LIX.*

Ormond Edward, *"Herodian Chronology", Palestine Exploration Quarterly 114 (1982) 29–42.*

Orosius, Adv. Pag. V1 22.7, V11.2.16 by Deferrari, R.J. The Fathers of the Church (Washington, D.C.: Catholic U. Press, 1964, Vol. 50, p. 281, 287). Vol. 50, p. 281, 287.

Ovid, (Res Gestae 35; Ovid, Fasti 2, 129).

Pratt, John P., "*Yet Another Eclipse for Herod*," The Planetarium, Vol. 19, No. 4, Dec. 1990, pp. 8-14.

Quarterly Journal of the Royal Astronomical Society, *"The Star of Bethlehem -- a Comet in 5 BC -- and the Date of the Birth of Christ,"* (1991).

Ratzinger, Joseph (Pope Benedict XVI) The Infancy Narratives – Jesus of Nazareth.

Setterfield, Barry, DVD: *The Christmas Star: Do Astronomy and History Support the Bible?* (produced by Freedom Films and Video).

Vardaman, Jerry; Yamauchi, Edwin M., eds. (1989). "The Nativity and Herod's Death". Chronos, Kairos, Christos: Nativity and Chronological Studies Presented to Jack Finegan (Winona Lake, Indiana: Eisenbrauns): 85–92.

Whiston, William, *The Complete Works of Josephus*, Kregel Publications, Grand Rapids, MI, 1981).

Zimmerman Jones, Andrew, The Star of Bethlehem - a Physics Overview of the Star of Bethlehem.

****

The Star of Bethlehem: The New Evidence
John C. Iannone

CPSIA information can be obtained
at www.ICGtesting.com
Printed in the USA
BVHW040255081221
623496BV00016B/1252